Memoirs of a Born Free

Memoirs of a Born Free

Reflections on the New South Africa by a Member of the Post-Apartheid Generation

Malaika Wa Azania

foreword by Simphiwe Dana

Seven Stories Press

New York • Oakland • London

Seven Stories Press
140 Watts Street
New York, NY 10013
www.sevenstories.com

Library of Congress Cataloging-in-Publication Data

Names: Malaika wa Azania, author. | Dana, Simphiwe, 1980- writer of foreword.
Title: Memoirs of a born free : reflections on the new South Africa by a member of the post-apartheid generation / Malaika Wa Azania.
Description: First us edition. | New York : Seven Stories Press, 2018. | "First published by Jacana Media (Pty) Ltd, 2014. Introduction " 2018 by Malaika Wa Azania. First US edition published by Seven Stories Press in July 2018."
Identifiers: LCCN 2018045389| ISBN 9781609806828 (pbk.) | ISBN 9781609806835 (ebook)
Subjects: LCSH: Malaika wa Azania. | Young adults--South Africa--Biography. | Youth, Black--South Africa--Biography. | Post-apartheid era--South Africa--Biography. | Blacks--South Africa--Social conditions. | Social change--South Africa. | South Africa--Social conditions--1994-
Classification: LCC DT1972.M335 A3 2018 | DDC 968.07092--dc23
LC record available at https://lccn.loc.gov/2018045389

Printed in the USA

9 8 7 6 5 4 3 2 1

This book is written for Mwalimu and Lalibela, the son I will one day mother and the niece in whose eyes I see the possibility of Azania unoccupied . . .

Contents

PART I
Born free? The conditions of growing up
in the Rainbow Nation

PART II
A kindled flame: Searching for a political home when the centre no longer holds

Introduction to the US Edition

IT HAS BEEN FOUR YEARS since *Memoirs of a Born-Free* was
first published in South Africa. So much has happened since
then. And while I remain the same young black woman who
is committed to the struggle for justice for black people in a
country that continues to deny us our humanness, I am also a
different person. A lot has happened in four years, and though
some events have bruised me in unimaginable ways, some have
strengthened my belief that another South Africas and indeed

another world, is possible. The #FeesMustFall protests that swept through the country in 2015 and 2017 were a watershed moment for our troubled democracy. I shall elaborate on that later.

I laid my mother to rest on the seventeenth of June 2017. She had passed away a week earlier after losing a brief but heart-wrenching battle with gastrointestinal cancer. She was only forty-five years old. Since her death, I have been struggling to find ways and time to deal with my grief. It probably sounds strange to hear a person say they do not have the time to grieve, but when you are a young black graduate from a working-class background, you begin to realise that grief too, like so many things in life, is a luxury that you simply cannot afford. At least not yet.

I was preparing for my mid-year exams when my mother fell ill. I had last seen her six weeks before—at my graduation for my undergraduate degree. Though a bit weak and unable to eat solid foods, she did not look to me like someone who was dying. I am not exactly sure how a dying person looks, but I would expect them to look less alive than my mom did. Anyway, for many years, she had been a health fanatic and at the time was a raw foodist. She was, in my view, the least likely candidate for death due to health reasons. But being a bit concerned, I suggested that she go get tested just in case her illness was more serious than it appeared. Within a few days, she had a diagnosis: gastrointestinal cancer. I would later find out that the doctor had informed her that the disease was terminal, and that she had less than three months to live. She died six weeks after the diagnosis.

I can distinctly recall the very minute that I knew my mother would die. It was just a few hours before she was pronounced dead—three days after being admitted at Leratong Hospital. On the eighth of June, while I was preparing for an exam the following day, the vice chancellor of my university, Dr Sizwe Mabizela, came to my apartment and asked me to postpone my exam and go see my mother. She had been admitted to hospital the day before, and indications from those back home were that she was slowly getting better. I wanted to write my exam—I believed, right until the moment I saw her lying in the hospital bed, that she would recover. I therefore did not see the need to miss an exam, and insisted that I would take the first flight out of the Eastern Cape Province after my exam. But the urgency in Dr Mabizela's voice convinced me to leave immediately, and within hours, my partner and I were on a flight to Johannesburg, paid for by a friend, Mary Metcalfe, who had been in contact with Dr Mabizela throughout the day.

Upon our arrival in Johannesburg, a friend drove us to the hospital, where I witnessed something that no child should ever have to see. My mother was lying in a hospital bed, comatose. But unlike the comas that one sees on television, where a patient is resting peacefully, my mother was shaking uncontrollably. I am not sure what was scarier: the involuntary movements that her body was making or the wide-open jaundiced eyes that were staring at me, with dried tears running down the cheeks. My mother, the strong and beautiful Dipuo Mahlatsi, was dying. The doctor informed me that they could not operate on the tumours that they had found in her brain (the cancer had metastasised) because she was in an advanced stage of kidney failure. Even without saying the words, I understood what the doctor was telling me: my mother was severely ill and there was absolutely nothing that they could do for her except watch her die.

My mom died a few hours after my visit. She never woke up from the coma. When my aunt broke the news to me over the phone (the hospital contacted her), I did not shed a single tear. I had wept uncontrollably, for hours, after seeing her. I had cried from the moment the doctor told me that we had to pray for a miracle, and fell asleep in a pool of my own tears. I knew when I left the hospital that the next time I would be there was likely to fetch her corpse. A part of me wished for that, because to lose her so suddenly was more bearable than to watch her suffer for many months and then eventually die. I am not a medical professional, but I knew that if she were to live, it would be a life of unbearable pain and indignity. My mother, vivacious and indomitable, would have most likely been in a vegetative state, dependent on dialysis and all kinds of invasive and painful treatment for her terminal cancer. Right before she fell into a coma, she had ceased to speak. What kind of life would the loud and talkative Dipuo have had if she had lost her ability to speak? How would we be able to take care of a terminally ill loved one when we barely had enough resources to survive? What damage would seeing my mother wither away have had on my fourteen-year-old brother, who has already been made fragile by an absent father who comes and goes from the child's life as he pleases? In many ways, my mom's sudden departure was a blessing. And yet knowing this does not make the pain less excruciating.

I knew as soon as I laid my mom to rest that grief was a

luxury I could not afford. I returned to university and negotiated that I complete my Honours degree in two months as opposed to five months. I could not be a fulltime student for five months—I needed to return to Johannesburg, the City of Gold, to find employment and take care of my sibling. My mom had been unemployed for many years at the time of her death, so she left us absolutely nothing. We barely had sufficient resources to bury her. I knew that my younger brother's life depended on me finding employment and stabilising financially. And so I buried myself in academic work, taking up as many modules as possible, and finding time to complete my dissertation. I was far behind. I had scheduled my field work and data collection for June—the month that my mother died. I was unable to do it, because funeral preparations took a week—the very week that I was supposed to be in rural Eastern Cape conducting interviews. For two months, I barely slept. I was lucky if I could manage four hours of undisturbed sleep. I had to finish my degree, I had to work for my brother. I did not have the time or the luxury to stay in bed for weeks and cry my eyes out—which is what I would have wanted to do. I wanted to cry for the immeasurable pain that the loss of my mother had brought. I wanted to cry for the woman who had sacrificed so much for me, and did not live long enough to see my grandchildren. I wanted to cry for so much—but it was not possible. My class background did not allow me to drown in my grief—a fourteen-year-old needed food to eat, fees to be paid, clothes to be bought and a sister to assure him that he would not starve.

I am one of very few lucky young black people in South Africa who found employment quickly. I do not underestimate my privilege in this regard, because when your country's official youth unemployment rate stands at a staggering 30 percent, then you know that it is not outside the realm of possibility that you too could be part of the statistics. And so now I wake up every morning to work, to put a meal on the table, because in a family where I am the only university graduate, no one else can. And so grieving is postponed—because I cannot afford to fall apart. My class position and the demands of black tax do not allow me to.

Since the first publication of Memoirs of a Born-Free South Africa has also gone through changes—most of them just as painful as my own personal loss. In many ways, we have lost a lot since 2014, not least of all, our faith as young black people in the capacity of our own democratically elected government to treat us as human beings who deserve dignity. The #RhodesMustFall and #FeesMustFall protests that swept through the country between 2015 and 2017 were a painful reminder to many of us that a state can and often does turn on its citizens.

Many who read Memoirs of a Born-Free in the year that it was published would not have been shocked at the events that followed just a year later, when students from historically White universities took to the streets in protest against the institutional racism that characterises the post-apartheid dispensation. They would not have been shocked because the book details how even in the new dispensation, the condition of native is still a nervous condition. As a twenty-one-year-old, I had tried to articulate the struggles of working-class black youths, to demonstrate how violent the legacy of apartheid continues to be. And in 2015, when the #RhodesMustFall movement ruptured the fragile fibre of the South African society and exposed its racism for the world to see, I felt vindicated, because even as some dismissed our legitimate experiences as sensationalist or dismissed us as being "stuck in the past", I had always known that this rupture was imminent. It was never going to be sustainable that the black majority could be perpetually rendered a cultural and economic minority in their own native land. Something had to give—and it did.

The #RhodesMustFall movement began at the University of Cape Town—one of the bastions of white privilege and black exclusion. For years, the institution had excluded black students, not only financially and academically, but culturally as well. The spatial injustice that characterises Cape Town was deeply pronounced through a spatial aesthetic that was as violent as it was deeply offensive. The University of Cape Town was a monument of apartheid and colonialism, physically and otherwise. Monuments in honour of imperialists greeted students as they walked through the campus, reminding black people that they did not belong. One morning, a group of students decided that this disregard for the long suffering of black humanity could not continue to be so boldly celebrated. With buckets of faeces as their weapons, the student activists desecrated the Cecil John Rhodes statue that had for decades welcomed students into the grounds of the University of Cape Town. This act of defiance marked the beginning of a journey that continues to characterise South Africa. All across the country, students stood up against institutional racism—physically removing monuments of our colonial past. Liberals and those who are irritated by the militancy of black youths argued that these monuments were an important symbol of our history, and should remain in place. No! we said. Take them to the apartheid museum where those who want to see them can visit them. Do not place them in public spaces as though they must be celebrated.

Some dismissed our actions as pointless. They contended that the desecration of colonial monuments would change nothing, in the bigger scheme of things. Those who expressed this simplistic analysis, devoid of any substance, failed to understand the depths to which such symbolism was liberating to students and black people in general. Desecrating the monument birthed a radicalism that had last been witnessed in South Africa during the 1976 student uprisings. This radicalism was not expressed only through acts of "vandalism", but in a new type of thinking that began to permeate all spaces. We were beginning to question the academic curricula that for a very long time they had accepted as normal. We realised that there was absolutely nothing normal about curricula that deliberately delegitimised certain voices—a curriculum that sustained itself through the pedagogical assault on black scholarship. There was nothing normal about a curricula that was deliberately designed to reproduce a reserve army of labour that is easily exploited. In realising this, we knew that it was not only statues of Rhodes that had to fall, but an education system that is in every way deeply problematic. From that point on, students engaged in a protracted struggle to transform and decolonise South African universities, both intellectually and physically. Doors of learning had to be opened.

In 2016, the #RhodesMustFall movement evolved

into a more radical movement that came to be known as #FeesMustFall. Having engaged in the struggle to decolonise the academy, we were now demanding access to higher learning institutions. In the democratic dispensation, black students from working-class families are still being excluded from universities due to financial constraints. Our class background is being used to mark us as undeserving of a chance to become better.

The #FeesMustFall movement started as a legitimate cause that had the moral authority to make demands on a government that had turned its back on the poor, and a private sector that did not understand that it had an obligation to contribute to nation building. In 2016, thousands of students across all South African universities took to the streets in protest against exorbitant tuition fees. Parents and businesses joined the students in these protests, forcing the government to declare that there would be no fee increase in the following year. But we were still dissatisfied, because our struggle was about lower fees. We wanted the government to declare free education and to erase historical debt for thousands of students who are unable to proceed with their education or to obtain their academic records due to outstanding fees. The government had to assure us that students who could not afford an education would be able to study, and that they would do so not on the loans that the government provides, which incur a lot of interest over time. Hundreds of thousands of black students are struggling to pay back their loans from the government, not only because the interest on these loans is unbearable, but because many of them are either unemployed or earn far too little to afford the monthly repayments—no matter how low such repayments may be. Many black students in the new South Africa are the first graduates in their families, and so the burden of taking care of everyone else falls on their small shoulders. Being the only university graduate in my family, the burden of building the family home, supporting my younger brother and other relatives and providing financial assistance to my ailing grandmother falls squarely on my shoulders. We refer to this as black tax—additional tax on top of the VAT and income tax that we already pay. This tax is unique to young black people who are beneficiaries of democracy, because it is we who have enjoyed some semblance of upward mobility, albeit minimally.

Over time, the movement disintegrated and with that, a criminal element began to emerge. Universities were being burnt down—sometimes by frustrated students, but often by young people whom the system had chewed up and spat out. Cracks began to appear within the movement itself. We were constantly at war amongst ourselves, and at the heart of the conflict was the deep-rooted misogynistic tendencies that characterised the movement. Men within the movement, accustomed to a heteronormative society that privileges their existence, viewed women and the LGBTIQ movement with extreme contempt. Some women believed, like Black Panther activist Elaine Brown once argued, that there is no revolutionary heaven where perfectly revolutionary men are created. These women argued that the #FeesMustFall movement needed to teach men feminist politics so that they could unlearn their misogynistic ways. But some women disagreed, and argued, legitimately, that male activists were unwilling to unlearn their patriarchy, and that it was bruising for women to constantly have to teach men how to treat women; how to recognise the humanity of women in the same way that they recognised their own. These internal differences, coupled with the extreme violence that the state was meting out on student activists, resulted in the weakening of the movement. The effects of the state's brutality on students will be felt for many years to come. The psychological damage that constant gunfire on our university campuses left on students is immeasurable. I distinctly recall the police opening fire on a group of students at Rhodes University, where I completed my undergraduate degree in 2016.

We were converged at the Steve Biko Union building, which despite its revolutionary name serves the conservative and racist interests of the Rhodes University brand. About a hundred students were discussing the way forward for the movement, which was slowly losing its moral authority as a result of the criminal elements that had gained a lot of ground. I recall very little about the moment that led to the police firing shots at us, but I remember very distinctly the piercing sound of gunshots and the suffocating smell of tear gas that had been used to disperse us. Everyone began to run, in many different directions. It was a chaotic scene straight out of footage of apartheid South Africa. I stood there—frozen. I could not move. No matter how much I willed my feet to move forward, they simply refused to. I was glued to the spot, confounded by the scene I was witnessing before my disbelieving eyes. As I stood there, transfixed, I saw a close friend of mine, Tiego Thotse, stumble to the ground like a sack of potatoes. The next thing I heard was a heart-wrenching scream, which turned out to be from a young woman over whom Tiego had fallen. As Tiego stood up to run, blood dripping down from his injured knee, the young woman remained on the ground—motionless. My boyfriend, who had been next to me when the shots were fired, came running towards me and violently yanked at my arm. All I remember after that was him and another comrade pulling me towards a tree for shelter. A few minutes later, we were running across campus, on our way to an apartment that we shared. Along the way, we came across Tiego and another student, Phunguphungu. Both of them were bleeding. Phunguphungu had been shot in the hand while trying to block a rubber bullet from hitting him in the face. His hand was so swollen that at first I thought he was carrying a rubber ball. Because my apartment was closest to campus, we decided to go there, where I had to administer first aid to the injured students. I had no idea what I was doing. In my state of shock and absolute terror, I had forgotten to even put on surgical gloves to protect myself. It dawned on all of us hours later that I had handled people's blood and we joked about how if I had contracted HIV/AIDS, it would be for a just cause. "You would have been infected in the struggle for liberation, Laika", Tiego quipped. It was surreal. I don't think I ever understood the depths of state brutality until that moment. Students were being shot all over the country, by private security and state police. But it had not yet happened at our university, and when it did, I realised just how vulnerable we were in the face of such violence.

The violence shocked and scared many of us. We knew that the state wanted to silence us, but we were unprepared for the extent it was willing to go to achieve this. The arrests that followed, and the endless court cases against students, coupled with the internal issues that I have mentioned, weakened the movement considerably. As the movement disintegrated, many students' resolve also weakened. The #FeesMustFall movement, two years after it was founded, effectively collapsed—and with it, the hopes and aspirations of millions of young black people who deserve a better deal than government has accorded them.

Whatever its faults and weaknesses, the #FeesMustFall movement created a necessary rupture that shook South Africa to its very core. For the first time in over two decades of its rule, the ANC-led government was confronted with students' power in ways that it never imagined it ever would be. For many years, we had been dismissed as a born-free generation, as beneficiaries of a democracy that to many of us, has been characterised by poverty, suffering and exclusion. It was a powerful moment for our country. Just like the Black Panther Party in the United States, the #FeesMustFall movement will live in the memories of both the oppressors and the oppressed, as a reminder that the human spirit eventually reaches a point where it can no longer accept to be treated as anything less than human. One day history will have its say, and it will speak of the thousands of young black South Africans who, when they could no longer breathe, when the weight of racism and inequality was pressing hard against their chests, rose up and said: NO MORE!

But before we were brave, before we dared to challenge the government, we were young, black, beautiful people who believed in the capacity of our leaders to do better than our oppressors did. We were the generation that was promised a better life. We were children of the ANC. But the revolution has a painful tendency to eat its young. We were bruised. But our stories must be told. *Memoirs of a Born-Free* is written by me, but it is the story of many of us. It is the story about what happens to a dream deferred—a story about what it means to be human in a world that is uncomfortable with a blackness that does not apologise or seek justification. It is a story about realising that liberators can and often do become oppressors. It is a story about what Joshua Nkomo so aptly captured, that "a nation can win freedom without its people becoming free". This is a story about the quest for freedom . . . and it begins in Soweto . . .

Acknowledgements

First and foremost, I want to thank my parents, Dipuo 'Stalin' Mahlatsi and Mike 'Gaddafi' Maile, for the love and support that you have given me throughout my journey of self-discovery.

To my sisters, Phindile Kunene, Tshepiso Mahlatsi, Thabile Maile, Mpho Mahlatsi, Lebogang Thokoane, Nkhensani Kubayi, Sarah Britten, Amanda Mbali Dlamini and Mamello Ntombela, thank you for believing in me when I had ceased to believe in myself.

To my big brothers, Sthembiso Khanyile, Sandile 'Saider'

Puti, Sibusiso Maneli, David Maimela, Tembile Yako, Mojalefa Motalane, Magasela Mzobe, Mzwandile Masina, Bomi 'Bomza' Mafanya and Ukho Botshiwe, thank you for your loving kindness and never-ending faith in my abilities.

To a team of involuntary mentors, Miranda Strydom, Mukoni Ratshitanga, Mary Metcalfe, Sello Pietersen, Phillip Kganyago, Lumka Oliphant, Nomfanelo Kota and Shane Maja, thank you for never running out of patience with me.

My sincerest gratitude to my editor, Natalie Gillman-Biljon, and my publisher, Thabiso Mahlape, who worked tirelessly to give coherence to my voice.

And, last but not least, a big thank you to you, dear reader, for believing that my story is important enough for you to read.

Foreword

I HAVE TAKEN A WALK THROUGH Malaika's life and found all of my own struggles—of course with slight variations in form and shape. I will not dwell on that. I have had the pleasure of engaging Malaika on a number of critical issues that affect the South African racial landscape. Never have I found such brilliance in one so young. I have watched her frustration with how the vision of a truly free South Africa seemed to dim every day. I have seen her lash out under the manipulations of those who, had they been truly for the struggle and not for themselves, should have nurtured her revolutionary spirit and seen her for the shining hope she is. I have wept for her as she lashed out at me under those very same manipulations. Sometimes I wished she and I had been born in the '70s, when the call for change was answered by a sincerity of action. So long I felt out of place in the black-on-black violence that we visit on each other because there is not enough space for all of us on the podium. Never mind that not all are worthy of the podium. The ego wants what it wants; worse a repressed ego. I have seen the growth of the cult and ego politics she speaks of and have slowly withdrawn to where I found myself all alone and deeply longing for political companionship. For long the word politics was a dirty word that I feared would corrupt me if I associated with it because I had seen what it has done to those who embrace it.

Though Malaika ends her monologue with a sentiment of hope, I find no hope in her words—only a lonely young woman who knows what needs to be done but whose ideals she can find no space for in the world she occupies. 'Africa eats her young'—these words scream at me as I carefully take a few steps into her mind, careful not to disturb anything. Yet I tumble into her thoughts, throwing everything into chaos. The chaos comes about because I suddenly remember that I am the Africa I speak of. That I am alone is a matter of perspective, if I shift my focus slightly I will find her impatiently waiting. Tortured by the agency that Africa has bestowed upon us. Because change is us. When I shift my focus, I find that there are certainly many of us. And that the struggle is a fog that threatens blindness. Nothing is as clear cut as it was for the youth of the '70s. Yet we must chart a path through the blinding and be careful not to step on our own in our enthusiasm for change. The fog has arrested our agency to a crawl and the impatience is killing us. This is the long walk.

I have since opened myself up to the patience of an unchartered climb and found many along the path. The many I used to look upon in contempt, because they were simply too slow; not radical enough. In the fog you have to dream with your eyes wide open. Open to the reality of a different and unfamiliar landscape, not to mention the blinding that is ever threateningly in your face.

Though we can learn from the past we do not live there anymore. The solutions of then sit uncomfortably within today's challenges. The game has changed and it necessitates that we change too if we are to be fit to serve not only the country but the continent, and find our place under the sun. These days have humbled us all. The enemy wears our face to confuse us. This is the long walk. So come my little sister, take a stroll with me. There is no need to rush; it will only quicken the burnout. Share the load, share the fear, you are not alone. At the end of our days only will we see that our labour for the struggle bore fruits every day. It is the fog confusing us, making us feel we are walking around in circles. Africa becomes freer every day because of you and I; take a pause and meditate on this. While at that, marvel at the beauty of the spaces we occupy—the rambling hills and green valleys. It is already ours, every day we take more and more of it back, even if it is just in the conviction of our words. We are no longer strangers in our own home. Never shall we be strangers again. One day you will see and that is the day you will truly smile. Take a stroll with me.

– Simphiwe Dana

april 2014

PART I

Born free? The conditions of growing up in the Rainbow Nation

A letter to the ANC

SINCE MY EARLY CHILDHOOD DAYS as a young girl growing up on the dusty streets of Meadowlands, I have wanted to write a letter to the African National Congress (ANC) to express my gratitude for the role it played in the liberation struggle. But there were other issues that I wanted to address, issues that have nothing to do with gratitude. I wanted to tell the ANC what life in the township is really like. I have been aching to describe to the ANC, for example, how it felt to make a transition from township schools into former Model-C schools, havens of classism and racism.

The only thing that prevented me from doing so was the anger that poured out of me every time I attempted to pen this letter. It was consuming and destructive and I knew that if I wrote a letter in that state of mind, it would not be constructive. And so I waited for a time when that anger had subsided, when I could write my reflections without spewing venom unnecessarily. And so here I am, finally ready to talk about the real face of the Rainbow Nation and the truth behind the so-called 'lost generation'.

I have heard many people speak about the 'lost generation' and of 'born frees'. It is said that children born in the early 1990s belong to the 'born-free' generation, a generation of those born after the end of the apartheid era. Children born in 1994 are said to have been born in times of equality, where racial privilege has been annihilated. I was born in 1991, exactly two years and six months before South Africa held its first democratic elections. By the time I came into being, the ANC and all other political organisations had been unbanned. Political prisoners, including Nelson Mandela, who would later become the first democratically elected president in the country, had been released. The armed struggle had been abandoned and the country was preparing for a negotiated settlement. It was a time of relative peace after many decades of endless war and suffering. And so, I too belong to the category of 'born frees', a problematic definition architected by those who want to keep our people blinded about the real face of the effects of colonialism and apartheid.

Many would have us believe that what transpired in 1994 was a revolution, but this is far from the truth. For a revolution to have occurred, the system would have to have been completely annihilated. The economics and politics of the revolutionised society would have to be an antithesis to the ones that defined the previous regime. But such did not happen in South Africa, where the same system that had given oxygen to the apartheid government continues to be in existence, to define the face of the republic. That system is capitalism, a brutal system that can only survive through the exploitation of the majority by the elite minority who owns the means of production, primarily, land. It is a system that necessitates that a labour reserve be created to sell to the elite, who, to maximise profit, must necessarily exploit the workers. It is a system that creates a welfare state so that the poor can remain indebted to the state that feeds them. It is a system that is both anti-poor and anti-majoritarian. In South Africa, it is also a system that is anti-black, because while the political breakthrough of 1994 deracialised governance, privilege and poverty continue to have a race: the former is white while the latter is black.

The South Africa that we see today is but a different version of yesterday's South Africa. It is a South Africa where racialism and racism are no longer imposed through violence in the raw sense of the word, nor are they constitutionalised as was the case during the apartheid dispensation. Racism and racialism are now institutionalised; they are the threads that hold together the fibre of South African society.

Those of us who have had the unfortunate 'privilege' of attending multiracial former Model-C schools have experienced firsthand what institutionalised racism means, because we are daily living in the boiling fire of white supremacy. Racism is institutionalised when a black child must wake up at an ungodly hour to take public transport to get to a 'good' Model-C school while a white child need only walk there or get dropped off by their chauffeur in a German-made car. Institutionalised racism is when there is no indigenous African language taught in primary schools and black students are forced to learn only English and Afrikaans, languages that are their third or fourth languages. By the time these students get to grade 10, where they have the option of choosing to do an indigenous language, they have been socialised into these languages and are hesitant to pick African languages for fear of failing. Model-C schools then argue that because few or no black students are willing to study a vernacular language it should be dropped from the academic curriculum, thus officially annihilating our indigenous languages in favour of Afrikaans and English. Institutionalised racism is when a black child's intelligence is measured by how well they can articulate in English when a white child's intelligence is not measured by how well they can articulate in Sesotho or isiXhosa. Institutionalised racism is when a black child's future depends on how well they understand *Macbeth*, a story completely divorced from their own experiences and reality. Our schools barely prescribe African literature. There is no Ngũgĩ wa Thiong'o in our prescribed readings. There is no Dambudzo Marechera, Mariama Bâ, Onkgopotse Tiro or Tsitsi Dangarembga. There is nothing at all that speaks to the reality of blackness. Institutionalised racism is when schools in the townships have no science laboratories or computer classes while students in former Model-C schools have limitless access to media centres and libraries stocked with excellent resources.

Institutionalised racism is when these students, those who have access to these resources, are accepted into universities where black students have the doors of learning shut in their faces. Institutionalised racism is when institutions of higher learning that are historically black, such as Walter Sisulu University, are being allowed to fall apart while ivory towers of white privilege, such as Rhodes University, continue to exist in vulgar wealth, operating similar to private schools. Institutionalised racism is a legalised form of modern-day apartheid. And it is a form of apartheid that the so-called born-free generation is subjected to.

The struggle of the generations before us, because of the period in which it happened, was a struggle for political freedom. It was a struggle for the attainment of basic human rights, chief among them the right for the people to govern. It was necessary that this struggle be waged, for without democracy as a foundation, neither revolution nor reform is possible. Democracy is impossible without political freedom but political freedom is not the ultimate objective of the revolutionary struggle. The ultimate objective is economic freedom, the liberation of the masses of our people from the clutches of economic bondage. But our people remain in chains. So, what about this generation, which has the mission of freeing the people from those chains, is 'free'? What about us is reflective of a 'born-free' generation when our generation is born during a time of the struggle for economic freedom and the quest for the realisation of the objectives of the African Renaissance agenda?

I may not have been born during times of constitutionalised apartheid but I still remain a product of an epoch of systematic, individualised and institutionalised apartheid. So nothing about me or those who were born after me is free. My story, my journey, is not a reflection of the freedom spoken about in the romantic speeches of government officials. It epitomises the ongoing struggle for liberation and for emancipation from mental slavery. And it begins in Soweto . . .

The beginning

MY NAME IS MALAIKA LESEGO SAMORA MAHLATSI. I was born twenty-two years ago in the now-dilapidated Meadowlands Community Clinic on a rainy morning on 19 October. It was my mother's twentieth birthday on that day. Her name is Dipuo Mahlatsi and, until just over a decade ago, she had dedicated her life to serving you: the ANC. Like me, she was born in the historical township of Soweto at a time when children could not have a childhood.

Dipuo's mother, Matshediso Mahlatsi, had been a young girl when she left her hometown of Parys in the Free State. Having been born into a poverty-stricken family, my grandmother was unable to attend school and, as a result, received no form of education. Like most young women from a working-class background in Parys, she had the responsibility of looking after the children of the many aunts and uncles who lived in the family home when they were out working the houses and gardens of white families. Cooking, cleaning and doing the laundry were also part of her responsibilities. The young woman, trapped in her own home, where she would have remained in a state of perpetual servitude, made the bold decision to leave the monotonous and stagnant life of the village in search of gold in Johannesburg: the city that never sleeps. In the late 1960s, alone and scared, my grandmother bid farewell to her displeased family and took a train to Johannesburg, where she would spend the rest of her life.

My grandmother has often narrated to me the story about her early days in the city. To this day, she remembers it as though it were yesterday. She tells me that the first sign that the train had entered Johannesburg was the smell of working men: men working underground to dig out gold they would never own, men weeding and watering the gardens of homes they could never enter and men running everywhere to evade the ruthless white policemen.

Johannesburg, she recalls, was a true concrete jungle. When she arrived in the city, my grandmother was completely alone. She knew she had some relatives somewhere in Soweto but she didn't know their exact location and didn't want to bother them with her unannounced presence. She was a beautiful young woman with nothing but a duffel bag containing her few possessions: two washed-out blouses, a black skirt that had been given to her by an aunt who had stolen it from a pile of her madam's old clothes, a single dress that she normally wore to church and two pairs of panties that today would be considered unfit for human wear. She had no money and no plans, only a strong desire to escape the suffocating realities of Parys. A woman who had been on the train with her from the Free State, realising that my grandmother was foreign to the city, offered to provide her with accommodation for a few days until my grandmother could sort herself out. Grateful for this intervention, she accepted and, on that night, slept peacefully on a thin mattress laid over a concrete floor in a small house in Moletsane, a township in the east of Soweto.

It was not too difficult to find work at that time. My grandmother, young, uneducated, desperate and black, was exactly the kind of worker the system wanted. She was soon working in the home of a white family as a 'girl', what we today call a domestic worker. The responsibilities of a 'girl' were no different to what she'd been doing back home: cleaning the house, doing the laundry and looking after children, this time of the baas and madam. Of course, this time around, she was remunerated for her work, albeit with meagre wages that could barely cover her living expenses. Now that she was working, it was expected of her by the lady who'd taken her in that she would contribute to the expenses of the house. At this point, my grandmother couldn't afford to rent a shack of her own so she continued to live with the family that had shown her kindness in a city known for its cruelty.

Over the next few years, my grandmother worked for the white family and continued to make ends meet with the little she was receiving. It may not have been difficult to find work at that time but whichever work a black person found, he or she was bound to find him- or herself being super-exploited. But the alternative was more terrifying and so black people found themselves working long shifts for peanuts, at times not even making enough to feed their families for a full month.

Towards the end of the 1960s, my grandmother met a young man. According to what she tells me, it was love at first sight. Having never had the opportunity to interact with young men around the township due to her busy work schedule, she hadn't had the time even for casual dating. But when she met this young man with his sun-kissed skin and charming mannerisms, my grandmother was swept off her feet and, before long, she was being courted by him. The relationship intensified with time and a year later she was carrying her first child by him. While very excited by this news, she was also terrified about the implications. She was unmarried and was hardly making enough money to be able to find a place of her own. It was already burdensome on the family she lived with that she was occupying what little space they had to themselves, and now she'd be bringing in an extra person to occupy yet more space. Her child's father was living with his family in the family home and so, like her, had no place of his own. Being unmarried, however, was a huge scandal, for which she knew her family back in the Free State would never forgive her. Back then, it was taboo for a woman to have a child out of wedlock. It would bring great shame to the family. But my grandmother wanted this child and she loved its father most dearly.

A few months into the pregnancy, her boyfriend asked her to move in with him and his family in another section of Moletsane. Relieved of the burden of having to explain her condition to the woman in whose house she was staying, my grandmother gladly moved to the Mokhethi home, where she received a warm welcome. She continued to commute to and from work on a daily basis until she was no longer able to do so. My uncle, Lesley Mokhethi, was born in 1969. Soon after his birth, my grandmother was back at work scrubbing the floors of white homes and looking after 'klein baases' and 'klein madams'. The Mokhethi family doted over the newcomer to the family. He was the first grandson of maMokhethi, the mother of my grandmother's boyfriend. All the women in the house took turns looking after him when my grandmother was at work. At night when she returned, feeling very lethargic, she would breastfeed him while she rested on the couch until both of them fell asleep. She would wake up in the early hours of the morning, often because of the piercing cold, to find that one of the aunts had covered her with a warm blanket and taken Lesley to bed. This would happen on days when her boyfriend would not have slept at home. On days when he did, he'd wake her up and take her to sleep beside him on a mattress laid on the concrete dining room floor. She never complained. It was not too unusual for a man not to sleep at home, and a good woman knew to not ask questions about his whereabouts when he returned.

By the time Lesley was just over a year old my grandmother was pregnant with another child. Having long since welcomed my grandmother as their son's prospective wife, the Mokhethi family was once again thrilled at the idea of raising the child in their home. But this excitement was not shared by the child's father, who was disputing the unborn child's paternity. Nonetheless, my grandmother continued to stay in the Mokhethi home until she gave birth to a healthy baby girl in October 1971. The child's looks gave its father more reason to deny it was his. The Mokhethi family was very light in complexion as a result of its partly white lineage. My paternal grandfather had been a product of a mixed-race pairing—a white man and a black woman. But this child was darker in complexion than even my maternal grandmother, and stuck out like a wildebeest on a busy city street in the Mokhethi family. That child was named Dipuo, which means 'a child born amid talks'. Unlike the first child, she did not assume the Mokhethi surname. Instead, she used her mother's: Mahlatsi. The talks and suspicions about the child's paternity became unbearable until, a few years later, my grandmother decided she'd had enough.

On a cold June morning in 1975, she packed her and her children's bags. She was determined to leave the Mokhethi household and raise her children on her own. Before she could walk out the door, she was stopped by their grandmother, who demanded that she leave on her own without the children. She knew that my grandmother had not informed her family about the birth of either child so it was very unlikely that she would be returning to the Free State. She also knew that my grandmother was not making enough money to be able to afford to rent a place of her own. But my grandmother refused to leave her children behind. She wanted them with her even as she knew not where she was heading. This led to an argument between her and the children's grandmother and, eventually, a cruel compromise was reached: my grandmother would leave her son behind and only take with her the daughter whose paternity had been the foundation of the conflict in the family. MaMokhethi would have wanted it differently but my grandmother was adamant that her daughter would be better off with her than with the family of a man who didn't even want her. The deal sealed, my grandmother took off with her daughter strapped tightly to her back, never to set foot in the Mokhethi home again.

Because she was not very familiar with Soweto even at that point, due to never having had a social life, my grandmother had no way of knowing just how close she was to the home of the relative she knew she had in Soweto. And so, after leaving Moletsane, she roamed the township in search of a place to rest her head. She walked for hours on end, knocking on doors, begging for a place for her and her child to sleep. Eventually, she found rescue in the form of a family that lived just outside Moletsane, where she had by now spent many years. For the next few months she lived happily with her newfound family while continuing to work 'at the kitchens', as working in white suburbs is called in the township. Her daughter was growing into a clever young girl, inquisitive and ahead of her peers. It was around this time that my grandmother began to search for her relatives. She eventually found them residing in Meadowlands Zone 3, just a few minutes away from Moletsane. By the time she moved in with them, she had two children with her: my mother and a son named Godfrey Motsamai Mahlatsi, who would die a painful death in 1999.

Life in Zone 3 was not much different from life in Moletsane. My grandmother was still forced to work in order to feed her children. She was not making a lot of money but having the burden of paying rent eased off her stretched far what little wages she earned from her work in the kitchens. My mother and Godfrey grew alongside the other children in the house and lived the ordinary lives of ordinary township children. By that time, they were both in primary school not too far from the family home. My grandmother had not seen Lesley in years and every night before she went to sleep, she would pray for his safety and for the Lord to have mercy upon her beloved children.

———

A few years went by.

The apartheid regime was unleashing brutality on the townships and when children were not on the streets kicking torn soccer balls, they were indoors locked away from the screaming police sirens and all-too-common petrol bombs that had become part of the township scenery.

In 1979 and 1981, my grandmother gave birth to another two sons: Vincent Teboho and Alpheus Liphapang Mahlatsi. They too, like my mother and Godfrey, grew up in Meadowlands Zone 3. A few years after the birth of Ali, as the youngest of the boys was called, my grandmother was on the move again. This time she relocated to Zone 8, where she spent her first few years staying with the Makama family, whose matriarch, known only as 'Mawe', she was very close friends with.

Dipuo, Godfrey, Vina (the nickname by which Vincent would be known for the rest of his life) and Ali were all attending school in Meadowlands. By then, Dipuo was in junior secondary at WK Maponyane in Zone 9 while Godfrey, Vina and Ali were all in Lejoeleputsoa Primary School in Zone 3. The three boys walked the ten-kilometre trip to Zone 3 every day. It was not unusual at the time. Schools in Soweto were, as they continue to be, very tribalist in posture, reflective of the tribalist posture of the township itself. Schools in zones 7, 8 and 9 had Setswana as the medium of instruction. All the primary schools—Tshimologo, Palesa, Retlile, WK Maponyane, Nkwe and so on—and all the high schools—Mokgome, Kelokitso, and so on—were for Setswana-speaking students. Schools in zones 1, 2 and 3 were mainly for Sesotho-speaking students. Lejoeleputsoa Primary School was one such school and because the Mahlatsi family was Sesotho-speaking, all the children attended it. My mother, being a highly intelligent child, had no trouble at all learning new languages and so it wasn't too difficult for her to switch from a Sesotho-medium to a Setswana-medium school.

A few years after moving into the Makama home, my grandmother was finally able to afford to rent a one-roomed shack, where she moved with her children in the mid-1980s. By this time, her only daughter, my mother, was a rebellious teenager heavily involved in student politics. Dipuo had graduated from WK Maponyane and was now studying at Kelokitso Comprehensive Secondary School, one of the oldest high schools in Meadowlands. She'd been bitten by the activism bug and was unstoppable in her political activities. This made my grandmother very angry but she knew there was absolutely nothing she could do to prevent her daughter from being an activist. Among other things, the material conditions of the time dictated that young people actively join the struggle to overthrow the apartheid regime that was terrorising and killing many black people.

The year was 1985 and a state of emergency had been declared nationwide. This signalled the increase in state repression. The Congress of South African Students (COSAS), which Dipuo had joined immediately upon entering high school, was banned in this year and township schools were being occupied by the police. Barely a teenager at this stage, my mother was among the many students who were detained by the police for leading boycotts. These were a form of resistance and along with consumer boycotts were a response to your call, ANC, to render the country ungovernable. You had made this call at the Kabwe Conference in Zambia when it declared a people's war as a tool to heighten mass action against the repressive regime.

My grandmother tells the story better. She remembers the day vividly, for it is etched in the gallery of her mind. She'd got off a taxi from work on a Friday afternoon and was looking forward to spending time at home with her children. By this time she was a cleaner at Kagiso Trust. It was the best job she'd ever had, she says. Kagiso Trust is an organisation that was established in 1985 as a mechanism to channel funds into programmes intended to help the oppressed fight against the apartheid regime. On Fridays she knocked off from work relatively early and, as a result, arrived early at the township. She always looked forward to this day, not only because she could spend time with her children but also because it was one of only two days in the week when she had the time to cook for them. During the week, because work ended late and taxi queues from town were long, the responsibility of cooking was left to my mother, who would return from school in the afternoon and cook before setting off to do her political duties. On Fridays, she made spykos for her children: potato chips with fried chicken and whatever fast food she managed to purchase from vendors in town. The children always looked forward to this meal. Fried chicken and potato chips were considered a great luxury in the township and whenever the children ate it they felt like royalty.

Kelokitso Comprehensive Secondary School also closed early on Fridays; both the teachers and the students were exhausted by the time the week ended. On Fridays, Dipuo would usually arrive home no later than two o'clock. The distance from school in Zone 9 to home in Zone 8 was no more than a twenty-minute stroll. There, she would complete her homework and assignments and then cut the potatoes into chips and leave them in a bucket for my grandmother to fry when she arrived home from work. She did this religiously before heading out to engage in her political activities. On that significant Friday afternoon, however, my grandmother returned home to find the potatoes uncut. This didn't worry her much. While her daughter was never neglectful of her household chores, my grandmother understood that from time to time children had to be allowed to stray a little. But by the time the sun set and my mother had not returned from school, my grandmother began to worry. Panic engulfed her as she went out into the streets to ask neighbourhood folk about her daughter's whereabouts. No one seemed to have the answer.

Later that night, after she had searched everywhere possible for her daughter, my grandmother was sitting with her three sons, all in a sombre state, when there was a knock on the door. Expecting it to be my mother, my grandmother jumped up and ran to the door, only to find herself face to face with a young man she didn't know. He introduced himself and told her that he was there to inform her of her daughter's whereabouts.

'Your daughter,' he said, 'was arrested this afternoon at school, along with other comrades.'

My grandmother was dumbstruck. Of course she knew that police were harassing activists and had made township schools their playing fields. And she also knew of many young people who had been arrested, never to be seen or heard from again. There were rumours going around that the police were killing people who were involved in political activities. They were not in any prisons, their bodies were in no mortuaries or hospitals and they had not crossed the border to join Umkhonto weSizwe (MK) or the Azanian People's Liberation Army (APLA) anywhere on the continent. Some were being thrown out of prison windows and their deaths reported as suicide. Some were being fed to crocodiles in the Zambezi River. The thought that her own child could be one of the statistics terrified her beyond measure. She thanked the bearer of bad news and returned to find her sons staring at the closing door, sitting in stunned silence.

Being a staunch believer in Christ, my grandmother dedicated the entire weekend to prayer. She pleaded with the Lord to protect her only daughter. She bargained with Him, vowed to be a better mother if only her daughter could be spared the brutality that she knew the police were capable of. But, more than anything else, she prayed for you, ANC. She prayed that someday you would be the ruling party so that children would cease to suffer. She prayed for all the children who were fighting for what you believed was the ideal South Africa. She prayed for the release of Nelson Mandela. She also prayed for white people to stop their hatred of black people.

A few days after that fateful night, my mother returned home with bruises all over her body and scratches on her face. Her clothes, or what remained of them, looked as though she had been involved in a violent fight with feral animals. My grandmother wasn't there when she arrived; she had gone to work with a heavy heart and a broken spirit. When she returned home from work that evening, pots were on the stove and the shack had been cleaned. Never before had she been as relieved as she was on that day when, just by entering the shack, she knew her daughter was home.

———

By the time she was in standard 8 (grade 10) in 1986, my mother was a seasoned activist of the Soweto Youth Congress (SOYCO) and being detained by the police had become part of her way of life. My grandmother had tried on numerous occasions to convince her daughter to cease her political activism. She'd pleaded until she no longer could, and threatened until she realised that she was fighting a losing battle. Dipuo was married to the liberation struggle and nothing anyone could say or do would convince her to abandon it.

But Dipuo wasn't the only one who was giving her parent a hard time. In the late 1980s, Soweto was the hub of student activism. In every township, young men and women, some barely teenagers, were involved in the activities of SOYCO and the United Democratic Front.

Many parents were living in constant fear that their own children would be victims of the cruelty of the police. They were terrified that someday their own children would vanish into the Zambezi River and never return home. So they did everything in their power to dissuade them from joining any political organisation or participating in any way in the struggle. But very few of the children did stop. They understood that the temporary discomfort of their parents was nothing compared to the permanent oppression of the black race by the apartheid regime. It had come to the point where something had to give: either apartheid was to be defeated or South African black people were to accept the demise of their civilisation. Apartheid was genocide and black people were perishing one by one. It had to stop. The children were going to stop it, with or without the blessings of their terrified parents.

Life in the township was becoming a living nightmare. Many students were not going to school, police presence had intensified since the declaration of the state of emergency in 1985 and victory was becoming more and more uncertain with every passing year. My grandmother continued as the matriarch of her family, raising her three sons and rebellious daughter, who was now hardly ever home. By this time, Vina and Ali were in senior primary school and their elder brother, Godfrey, was in junior secondary. They were excelling academically, like their older sister, and my grandmother prayed every day that they would not follow in her footsteps.

———•———

Towards the end of 1989, my mother announced that she was leaving Meadowlands and going to Alexandra, a township in the east of Johannesburg. Alexandra, one of the oldest townships in South Africa, was a haven for political activists. As you know, ANC members, most activists who later joined the Congress, including Nelson Mandela, had lived in this working-class township that today continues to reflect the brutality of class segregation. Alexandra was initially intended to house labourers who worked in the mines of the Witwatersrand area where, in the 1800s, gold had been discovered. Over the years, and with the heightening of the struggle, it had become a safe-house for political activists on the run from the police. Alexandra, because of its history of violence, terrified even the most hardened of police. Hardly any police patrolled the area, both because of the violence and the dense clustering of shacks. The latter made it almost impossible for activists who hid there to be found. This character of Alexandra made it an ideal place for activists and it was this that made Dipuo and many of her comrades descend on the township. My grandmother didn't protest when this announcement was made. By then she had reconciled herself to the reality that her teenage daughter was lost to the struggle and, above all, to you: the African National Congress.

My mother did not return home until January 1990, the year when Nelson Mandela was released from prison following the unbanning of political parties in the country. The apartheid regime was finally prepared to sit down for negotiations with national liberation movements and make a settlement that would see the end of the oppression of the black majority. The armed struggle had been abandoned to make allowance for peaceful talks. Students were back behind their desks and the streets of the townships no longer resembled a warzone. For the first time in many years, South Africa was alive with hope.

As a result of her education having been interrupted, by 1991, aged twenty, my mother was in high school completing her matric. A year prior to that, she had met a fellow activist who was leading COSAS in Soweto and had started a relationship with him. The young man was barely a year older than her and the relationship started off a whirlpool of childish romance in times of political instability. They usually met at COSAS meetings in Meadowlands, where he was also a resident. He was as assertive as she was, and theirs was considered a star-crossed relationship doomed to fail, not only because they were similar in so many ways but also because the political climate at that time made little allowance for such relationships to blossom. Student activists were perpetually on the run from the police, forced into hiding in townships like Alexandra. More often than not, even their parents wouldn't know their whereabouts, for they had to live as silently as thieves in the night if they were to be able to elude the vigilant eyes in the patrolling police vehicles that guarded the townships like hawks. But this relationship wouldn't meet its fate without leaving a permanent mark of its existence. Sometime after they met, the two lovers were expecting a child.

My mother maintains to this day that she was unaware of her pregnancy. She claims there were hardly any symptoms to indicate that a foetus was growing inside her uterus. Not until she was five months into the pregnancy did she know that she'd be bringing a child into the world. But when the knowledge presented itself she nevertheless, without any income and being out of school, made the decision to keep the child—a light in the dark odyssey of apartheid.

On 19 October 1991, Malaika Lesego Samora Mahlatsi was born at the Meadowlands Community Clinic, weighing a healthy three kilograms. It would be eleven years before my mother would have another child, whom she would name Morena Lumumba Rethabisitswe Mahlatsi, after the former prime minister of Zaire, Patrice Lumumba, a son of the soil who was snatched away from the arms of mother Africa far too soon.

The 'born free'

I WAS BORN IN INTERESTING TIMES. A year before my birth, apartheid laws had been relaxed by FW de Klerk, the then president of South Africa. As I've mentioned, this meant that political parties, which had been banned following the gruesome Sharpeville Massacre in 1960, were unbanned. Political prisoners were also freed, including Nelson Rolihlahla Mandela, an anti-apartheid campaigner and leader of your organisation. Mandela had been convicted of treason and sabotage in June 1964 and sentenced to life imprisonment. But on 11 February 1990 at quarter past four in the afternoon, Mandela appeared at the gates of Victor Verster Prison in Paarl in the Western Cape with his beautiful wife, Mama Winnie Madikizela-Mandela, by his side. He was a free man after spending almost three decades incarcerated.

My mother often tells me about this moment. She has repeated the story many times, always in a very emotional state. This is the story in her words:

A short while before Nelson Mandela was freed from prison we received a message that he would be flown to Soweto to the Jabulani Amphitheatre on the day of his release. And so, just before the scheduled day, 11 February 1990, leaders of COSAS and other organisations mobilised their members to fill up the arena at the Amphitheatre and welcome the struggle hero.

The day finally came. I remember vividly that it was a Sunday. Hundreds if not thousands of us walked all the way from Meadowlands to Jabulani chanting revolutionary slogans. Just before we arrived, at the time scheduled for his release, something extraordinary happened. It began to rain heavily. This was no ordinary rain. It was the kind that announces itself with roaring thunder and pours down hard, almost as if the heavens are weeping. By the time we arrived at the small venue, we were soaked. But we were all so excited and so loud in our singing and chanting that no amount of rain could have persuaded us to run for cover.

A few minutes after our arrival, one of the ANC leaders, I think it was comrade Popo Molefe or Terror Lekota if I am not mistaken, made an announcement to the large crowd that Mandela would not be coming on that day, that we were to return home and meet the following day at FNB Stadium.

The crowd dispersed and, in that torrent, we chanted back home, disappointed but not angry.

The following day, on a warm Monday morning, an even bigger group from Meadowlands met at Mapedi Community Hall in Zone 2. We marched again, this time to FNB Stadium just outside Diepkloof. There were all kinds of people: students in their uniforms, workers, the unemployed and every other person who lived in the township. When we arrived at FNB Stadium it was almost full to capacity. On top of that, the roads leading to the entrances were blocked. Everywhere one looked, there were people holding up posters with slogans like: 'Free at last!' and 'Welcome home, Madiba!'

Eventually, in the midst of all the singing and the chanting, he arrived, with Mama Winnie Mandela at his side. You could see on his face that he was stunned. The atmosphere in the stadium was electric! Mandela even lost balance and had to be held by other comrades. The stadium was shaking as we were singing one particular song. The words go like this:

Nelson Mandela!
Sabela uyabizwa (uyabizwa) Sabela uyabizwa!
Wena Madiba!
Sabela uyabizwa (uyabizwa) Sabela uyabizwa!

We were so loud that at one point comrade Popo Molefe, yes it was him, took the microphone and pleaded with us to calm down. He informed us that the stadium had recently been built and if we kept on stomping our feet like we were doing, the concrete panels would fall off. But no one listened to him; we were in a frenzy. We all wanted to have a glimpse of this man, Nelson Mandela, who for many years we had heard of. For years, we were taught about him in our political education sessions and we knew that part of our fight was for his release so that he could come and lead us into a new South Africa. We all wanted to just see him, however briefly.

He was brought up to the podium to speak to the crowd and when he did, the humility oozed out of his trembling voice. He said he knew while he was incarcerated that there were many people outside who were supporting him, but had not realised until that moment just how many these people were. He told us that he was shocked and then ended by thanking the country for the support and the commitment to the struggle. That was the birth of a new dawn. At that moment, I believed without a shadow of a doubt that the African National Congress, my organisation, would rule the country for a very long time to come . . .

The warm Saturday morning I was born was a year and eight months after that historic day of Mandela's release. The Nationalist Party was still in power but everyone, including white people, knew its grip on political power would draw to an inevitable end sooner rather than later.

Three days after my birth, my mother took me home to her family in a one-roomed shack that she shared with my grandmother and four of my mother's siblings. The fourth and last born, Tshepiso, had been born eight months previously at Baragwanath Hospital, usually called Bara, in Diepkloof. Tshepiso had had an identical twin but three months after their birth baby Tshepang had died from asthma. Tshepiso was also a sickly child and spent most of her early childhood hospitalised. As a result of this, my mother had to look after me without the assistance of her mother. On top of that, she had to look after her younger brothers. But by then they were relatively independent, save for their reliance on their older sister to cook and keep the house together while my grandmother was juggling frequenting Bara and work at the kitchens.

I had a normal childhood by township standards. Like all the other kids in the neighbourhood, I played on the dusty streets and attended day care not too far from home. By the time I was five years old, Tshepiso was out of hospital. We were inseparable, and would be for many years to come.

Township education

I WAS SIX YEARS OLD when I started school at Tshimologo Junior Primary in Meadowlands Zone 9. Back then, a law had been introduced that children younger than seven years old could not be in grade school but because of my inquisitiveness and unusual sharpness, I was allowed into the school. However, because of my age and the fact that I would be turning seven after June, I was placed in a grade 0 class that was mainly intended for six-year-olds who would turn seven before June. Tshepiso was placed in a grade 1 class.

By this time my mother was working full time as an admin

assistant at the Research Triangle Institute, a North Carolina-based non-governmental organisation (NGO) that was sub-contracted by the US Agency for International Development in Pretoria to implement a project dealing with human rights issues. My grandmother was still employed by Kagiso Trust as a cleaner and all my uncles were in high school. Because of this, there would have been no one at home to take care of us if we hadn't been in school. Although my mother was making relatively good money at her job, most of it was spent on paying school fees for all of us and for her fees for the University of South Africa, where she was studying towards a Bachelor of Arts degree majoring in Communications and Literature. As a result, there was no money to pay a babysitter. Tshepiso and I returned from school and Ndivuvho, whose father was our landlord, was tasked with opening for us and ensuring that we had lunch, after which we'd go out to play in the streets until late afternoon, when my uncles returned home from school to look after us.

The medium of instruction at Tshimologo Junior Primary School was Setswana, a language Tshepiso and I had learned to master because of the friends we played with. Dipuo, Ntswaki and Lala were from the same family and all spoke fluent Setswana. Another one of our friends, Nhlanhla, was Xitsonga-speaking but had also assimilated into speaking Setswana. The six of us were thick as thieves. Ntswaki, Tshepiso and I went to the same school, so every morning we would walk together to and from school. Dipuo, Nhlanhla and Lala attended schools that were located in the same vicinity and, like us, walked to and from school together in the mornings and afternoons.

One thing I distinctly remember about Soweto in the early 1990s is that the people were in a perpetual state of euphoria. There was always something to be excited about and it often had to do with your organisation. Every second person was talking about something good that the ANC had done. People were becoming unrealistically superstitious; everything that occurred would be linked to you in one way or another. If a student passed, you'd get the credit. If a person who was ill got better, it was said you had some influence in that. One particular incident stands out. It was a very cold evening. Tshepiso and I were drawing and colouring in our school books. I was around five at the time. We were still living in the one-roomed shack in Zone 8. There were two single beds at home. Tshepiso and I shared one of them and my mother slept in the other. My grandmother slept in the small space between the two beds. She always maintained this was the best spot in the entire shack, because, she claimed, it was insulated and warm. Thinking back, I suspect she was saying this to put us at ease. My uncles, Vina, Ali and Godfrey, slept on the floor in the part of the shack that we had divided into a kitchenette and a dining room.

While we were going about our colouring business, my uncles and their friends burst into the house screaming excitedly about something to do with Bafana Bafana. Tshepiso and I were instructed to dress warmly and told that my mother would be coming to pick us up shortly. Sure enough, a few minutes later she burst into the house with her friend, Sibongile, whose mother, Mawe, my family had lived with in the 1980s. They took us both outside, where the first things I heard were cars hooting and people singing loudly. My mother explained to us that the national soccer team had won the Africa Cup of Nations and had just been crowned champions. We were taken to Maseru Street, one of the busiest streets in Meadowlands, where a large crowd had gathered to celebrate the victory.

The entire community had come out onto the streets. Everywhere I looked there were people of all ages singing, dancing and hugging one another. Music was blaring from the many cars that lined the street. Some cars were playing songs by MaWillies, a popular kwaito artist who lived just a few streets from my home, while others were playing Brenda Fassie, whose songs were national anthems in the township. It was an electric atmosphere.

After what felt like hours of singing and dancing, the crowd dispersed. People began to walk to their homes with a sense of jubilation.

'Bafana Bafana won because of the Madiba Magic,' many claimed.

It was a very happy time. Apartheid was now finally over. You were now in power and the word on everyone's lips was 'Nelson Mandela', who at that time was the president of the Republic of South Africa. It was not too unusual to hear young children singing on the streets:

Nelson Mandela! Nelson Mandela!
Ha hona ea tshoanang le ena!

We were all young and we all loved Mandela, the man who had liberated us from the clutches of apartheid brutality, the leader of the ANC, the party of black people, which all of us were expected to join when we grew older.

At school, we were taught only four things: religion, mathematics, reading and Mandela. Tshimologo Junior Primary School, like all other schools in the township, was very serious about biblical education. Every morning before we went to class, we were gathered at the quad for assembly, where Bible scriptures would be read out to us by different teachers before the principal made the announcements of the day. The first class of every morning was Bible class. We would sit on the floor around our teacher, Mistress K, and have Bible stories read to us. Sometimes she would delegate the task of reading to students, or rather, to me or my friend Boitumelo. Boitumelo and I were her favourites, primarily because we read very well.

I hated that class. For some reason, hard as I tried, I could not make myself like the Bible and its stories. Something about it all felt unrealistic, not so different from stories about Father Christmas and his reindeer bringing presents for little kids from some place far up in the sky. So, on days when I was instructed to read to my classmates, I'd read as quickly as I possibly could. This was made easier by the fact that I spoke very fast anyway. The only thing I looked forward to during these classes was the singing. I had always enjoyed Christian hymns. They were the sole reason for my going to church. Something about them moved me. One in particular, *Haufi le Morena*, touched the depths of my soul in ways that I still battle to comprehend. And so I'd rush through the New Testament so there'd be more time for singing.

I was a very inquisitive student, the complete opposite of my aunt, Tshepiso, who was a grade ahead of me. Teachers often compared me to my quieter relative, who had hardly any friends and only spoke when spoken to. I was especially interested in reading and history. I always read ahead of the class, so that by the time they were halfway through a prescribed reading book, I was starting another. History class, or what I call 'Mandela lessons', was one of my favourites. My teacher, Mistress M, was very passionate about teaching us about apartheid, mainly because this particular subject matter allowed her to speak about her favourite person on the planet, Mandela, and her favourite organisation, the ANC, endlessly. One morning, Mistress M came into class with a huge smile on her face. She explained to us something called Curriculum 2005. But, of course, none of us had a clue what that meant or even how relevant it was to us. This was around 2001. The year 2005 sounded like a lifetime away.

After her complex explanation of the Curriculum 2005 programme, Mistress M suddenly began to quiz the class about all sorts of things. But we knew most of the answers to her questions; we had listened attentively during her prior lessons.

'Who is the premier of Gauteng?' she asked.

'Mbhazima Shilowa!'

'Who is the premier of the Northern Province?'

'Ngoako Ramatlhodi!'

'Who is the premier of the Northern Cape?'

'Manne Dipico!'

'Who is the premier of North West?'

'Popo Molefe!'

This went on for some minutes. Then she asked, expectantly, 'Who is the Minister of Education?'

'Kader Asmal!'

Mistress M's mood changed immediately. She began barking at us, calling us all sorts of cruel names. I sat in my chair, frustrated. I knew we had been correct: Kader Asmal *was* the Minister of Education; we had been told that many times before. And as far as I knew, he had neither died nor been replaced by anyone else, for whatever reason. So why was Mistress so angry at us, claiming that our collective response was incorrect?

While I sat there trying to make sense of this, Mistress M started asking students one at a time what the correct answer to her question was. Student after student was being given two lashes with her wooden rod for giving an incorrect answer. Every 'It is Kader Asmal, Mistress', was followed with a hard thud as wood met flesh. I was petrified. She'd soon be standing before my desk and I too would give her the same answer that everyone else was giving her because I too knew the Minister of Education to be Kader Asmal. I knew I'd be the last student she'd ask. I always was. Teachers in my school believed that 'clever' students must be given the least attention. As such, my homework book was never checked and I was never asked questions because it was expected that my homework would be done and that I'd know the answer, so the others must first try to answer. Because of this, I'd never before been given a lashing. I'd been in Tshimologo Junior for almost four years by then but not once had I been a victim of corporal punishment. But I knew that day that I too was about to suffer the fate usually suffered by other students. I was terrified.

Mistress M finally stood before my desk, her wooden stick lowered because of the expectation that she wouldn't hit me. I could hear my classmates weeping all around me, their hands burning from being struck by the painful rod. She asked, with pride in her eyes as she looked at her shining star, who the Minister of Education was. I didn't respond immediately. I was terrified of the consequences. After what felt like decades, I finally answered, 'It is Mr Kader Asmal'. A few seconds after uttering that response, I knew I was about to be hit.

Mistress M lifted the wooden rod up and demanded that I stretch out my arm with my palm facing up. I complied. The pain that shot through my arm was like none I'd ever experienced. So severe was it that for a few seconds after I'd been struck, I was numb. My mind froze. I couldn't move or even think. When I came to, Mistress M was screaming at us, telling us how disappointed she was at our collective stupidity, which, according to her, we had inherited from our parents, products of Bantu education. The correct answer, she told us, was not Kader Asmal or Mr Kader Asmal. The correct answer was *Professor* Kader Asmal. A professor, she explained, was not just an ordinary person. It was someone who had studied for a very long time and had obtained many degrees. That is who the Minister of Education was. She made it a point to emphasise that the reason why we had a *professor* as a Minister of Education was that the ANC took education seriously.

'The ANC wants you to have education better than what we had during the dark days of apartheid,' she informed us.

This became a daily narrative for students at Tshimologo Junior. Every day was dedicated to extending eternal gratitude to those who fought for the liberation of black people: you.

We would be beaten if we forgot who the first president of the ANC had been or how many years Nelson Mandela had spent in prison. At times, as an adult, I find myself thinking that there must have been a moment during this period where the national anthem was almost altered to include Mandela's name. I am almost certain that somewhere in the corridors of power, someone sat contemplating the possibility of dedicating the anthem to Mandela, as everything else was being dedicated to him. Maybe the national anthem would have gone like this:

Mandela sikelel' iAfrica
Maluphakanyisw' uphondo lwayo,
Yizwa imithandazo yethu,
Tata, sikelela,
Thina lusapho lwayo.

Madiba boloka setjhaba sa heso,
O fedise dintwa le matshwenyeho . . .

Indeed, the mid and late 1990s were an interesting period. Life in Meadowlands was exciting. The streets were bustling with children playing diketo and bathi, with no worries about tomorrow, for we knew without doubt that our future was secure. The ANC was in power and nothing could ever threaten or destabilise your hegemony. At home, things were also going very well. My uncles looked happier than they had ever been. Ali, the youngest of the three, had taken to playing dice on the streets but not for lack of resources. My mother ensured that everyone in the house was well clothed and well fed. By this time, both Ali and Vina were studying at Kelokitso Comprehensive Secondary School in Zone 9, hardly fifteen minutes from home. The days of walking to Zone 2 were long gone.

My grandmother was very happy at her place of employment. She'd been promoted from a cleaner to making photocopies and doing other minor administrative jobs around the office. This had done wonders for her self-esteem. She walked around the house with a spring in her step, a clear indication that she was content with the direction her life was taking.

At school, both Tshepiso and I were performing very well academically. Since the first lashing I had gotten from Mistress M, I had been hit a dozen more times for other minor misdemeanours. I was still a diligent student but no longer interested in being the teachers' favourite. My fear of being punished had vanished on that morning when I'd received a cruel lashing for not having prefixed Kader Asmal's name with '*Professor*'. From that day, I had begun to allow myself to be a normal kid, to cease striving to be the innocent one. This decision opened up a whole new world for me. For the first time in my life, I could actually say the ludicrous things that my peers were saying, as opposed to the clever things I had learned from my mother. Strangely, the teachers were not very displeased with my evolution. I continued to be their favourite, only this time they knew to check my homework book as they did every other student's.

Unfortunately, during this epoch of euphoria and contentment, tragedy struck in my family. This incident would alter my thinking forever. Years later, I would begin to understand its relationship with the false idea of a 'Rainbow Nation'.

Only the good die young

I WAS EIGHT YEARS OLD when the tragedy struck my family. I still remember the day as vividly as if it was yesterday.

Towards the end of 1998, my family moved out of the shack in Sekhwiri Street, a place we had called home for over a decade. We moved into a four-roomed house, just a stone's throw from our former home, in Tlhomedi Street. For the first time in our lives we had our own house. A proper brick house! There were two bedrooms: one for the women and one for the men. My uncles slept in the smaller bedroom, which wasn't small at all. The master bedroom had one queen-sized bed and one single bed. Tshepiso, my mother and I slept on the bigger bed while my grandmother slept on the small one. A humongous wooden table took up most of the space in the dining room. Eight black plastic chairs surrounded it. These were enough for all of us to eat supper together. This had never happened before because we'd lived in a shack so small that we hardly had any room to move. A television set completed the furnishing in the dining room. It too was a first. We'd never owned a television. My mother used to watch it at her friend Sibongile's house and my uncles would watch it at the homes of their friends around the neighbourhood. The only time Tshepiso and I got to watch television was when we spent nights at our friends' homes.

Moving to Tlhomedi Street is one of the happiest memories of my childhood. We were no longer living in a shack that was boiling hot during summer and freezing cold during winter. The days of using a bucket to relieve ourselves at night were also long gone. We now had our own toilet just outside the house and the bedroom in which we slept was big enough that having a bucket placed inside at night to prevent our having to walk in the dark was not as uncomfortable as it had been back in Sekhwiri Street, where we had to jump over the heads of those sleeping on the floor to be able to get to the bucket. The new house was also close enough to the old one that we could still keep the same friends we'd had throughout our childhood. Every morning, Tshepiso and I walked a block to Sekhwiri Street to fetch Ntswaki so that we could walk to school together. By this time, Dipuo had also started attending a school closer to our own, so she too walked with us in the mornings and waited for us in the afternoons.

They would arrive home and change while we waited for them and then walk with us to our new home, where we too would change into casual clothes and wash our socks and shirts. From then on, we would all eat either at my home or at theirs. We preferred eating at Tlhomedi, as we called my home. My grandmother often brought leftover food from her office whenever there were workshops or meetings, and my mother also bought nice food for us. Our fridge always had cheese and polony: the delicacy of the township.

Our house was always full of people: either our friends or my uncle's friends, who also came to eat at our house after school. On weekends, my mother would sometimes host what she called a 'kitchen party' with her friends. They would bring salads and snacks, and sit in the garden the whole afternoon dancing and singing along to Brenda Fassie's music.

When school closed, my mother, my grandmother, Tshepiso and I often went to visit our relatives in the Free State. My grandmother had since reconciled with her mother and the rest of her maternal family. So my family vacationed in Parys or in Kroonstad in the Free State, a place I continue to call home. My uncles were not particularly fond of the Free State; they argued that it was too rural. This attitude was typical of youngsters growing up in the township. Everything that was not similar to township life was either too rural or boring. Not that I particularly disagreed with them; Kroonstad and Parys were indeed very foreign to the life that we were used to in Soweto. We would be woken up very early in the morning to fetch water at a well almost an hour away from home. Upon returning, one of the older girls would prepare breakfast while the rest of us swept the yard and fed the chickens. One of the boys would start a fire and boil a lot of water, which was used for bathing and making tea. After eating breakfast, dishes would be washed and then we'd go out into the wild to play. At times while playing in the bushes, we'd find and kill small snakes and other animals. At times we'd go to the river to swim, without so much as swimming costumes. We would then head back home before sunset, when the older girls would prepare supper. After that, we would sit around a bonfire and listen to one of my great grandmothers, Motjholoko, tell us stories about the past. I enjoyed being in the Free State. The tranquillity of life in the rural areas resonated well with my spirit. I always looked forward to vacation time.

For some reason I never understood, we didn't go to the Free State during the March holidays of 1999. We remained in Meadowlands with our friends, who hardly ever went anywhere for vacation. The month passed without incident. Life in the township was normal. Vina and Ali were always out on the streets with friends. Ali was still playing dice and sometimes when he won a lot of money he'd give Tshepiso and me a rand each. A rand was a lot of money at that time. It could buy a packet of sweets, biscuits and sweetened ice, which sold for ten cents for one. Godfrey was hardly ever home but when he was the house would be filled with laughter and joy. He had long since dropped out of school and we were never told where he was staying or what work he was doing to survive. But whenever he came back, he'd bring all of us lots of gifts: clothes, jewellery, electrical appliances and food that we'd only ever seen on television. And every time, just before he left once again, he'd promise to take Tshepiso and me to

'Never-never', a place with golden streets and furniture made of different kinds of chocolate.

A few months before March 1999 something strange happened. It was an unusually chilly night in late January and we had all gone to sleep early because of the piercing cold. As usual I was nestled between my mother and Tshepiso. Some time in the middle of the night there was a banging sound at the gate of our house. My grandmother woke up and, with Vina walking closely beside her, went to open the gate. It was the police. My mother, who had also heard the commotion, woke Tshepiso and me immediately and told us to pretend to be sleeping until the police woke us up. When they did, she said, if they pointed at Godfrey, who had been sleeping at home that week, and asked who he was, we should say 'ab'ti Thabiso'. We did as instructed: tucked ourselves back into the warm blankets and tried with all our might to pretend to be asleep. We could hear voices in the kitchen, which slowly moved through the rooms, stopping first at Ali and Godfrey's room and interrogating them. The next thing I knew, there was loud banging on our door and a torch was being shone around the room. Someone must have located the light switch in the dark because a few seconds later the light came on. The three bulky, angry-looking police officers yanked the blankets off our tiny bodies. We sat up with a mixture of terror and anticipation. Rubbing the sleep from our eyes, we stood beside our family members and awaited the imminent interrogation. The officers asked us to identify our family members by name. They pointed to my grandmother first, and we responded with 'Mama'. Next, they pointed at my mother, to which we responded 'Puo', which is what we called her. They went on, pointing at Vina and Ali, and our responses were simultaneous. The last person they pointed to was Godfrey, who had a slight look of fear in his almond-shaped eyes. But we knew what we had to say and were determined to say it convincingly. 'Ab'ti Thabiso,' we stated matter-of-factly.

The look of confusion was evident on the officers' faces. We were children and they couldn't interrogate us further, and it must have seemed ludicrous that we could have been involved in a cover-up. In his usual disarming voice, Godfrey asked the officers who they were looking for at such an ungodly hour, and why. An officer responded that they were looking for a young man named Godfrey, wanted in connection with a murdered police officer and a stolen vehicle. They'd received an anonymous tip that he lived in this house and were there to arrest him. Godfrey calmly assured them that no such person lived at our house and, followed closely by my grandmother in her blue blanket and slippers, escorted the frustrated police officers out.

After the police officers left, none of us could get back to sleep. The tension in the house was as thick as a blanket. I was confused by the incident, battling to comprehend what the police officers had given as reasons for their manhunt of Godfrey. My grandmother looked as though she'd aged ten years within the few minutes of the incident. Tshepiso and I were instructed to return to sleep while my mother and grandmother held a brief meeting with Godfrey. The very next day, we woke up to find Godfrey packing the little that there was of his clothes and luggage. He kissed us goodbye and promised he'd come back and take us to Never-never.

———•◦•———

On 30 March 1999, I was visiting my paternal grandmother in Meadowlands Zone 1 when my mother came with her partner, abuti Bathandwa, to pick me up and take me back to Zone 8. I was asked to wait in my father's room while the elders had a discussion that, judging by their body language and facial expressions, looked very serious. I don't recall how long I waited but at some point I went out and met him as he was heading towards the room. All he said to me was, 'Godfrey o shwele. Ba mo thuntse a nkela maponesa dithunya.'

I froze in my tracks. What my father had just said made very little sense to me. 'Godfrey is dead. He was shot while trying to disarm police officers.' This was impossible. My favourite uncle could not possibly be dead. The last time I'd seen him had been the day after being woken up by the police in the middle of a cold night. As far as I knew, he had gone to rural Free State to stay with our family, away from the probing eyes of the police. So why was he killed? Where?

That night, I sat on my mother's lap as abuti Bathandwa drove us back home. My mother was trying very hard to be strong for me but I could tell that a tsunami of tears was threatening to pour out of her red, swollen eyes. The ten-minute drive from Zone 1 to Zone 8 felt like a lifetime. The car was eerily silent, save for the sound of screeching tyres against tar. I was still battling to comprehend how it was possible that Godfrey could be dead. He had promised to take us to Never-never. He had no right to just die without fulfilling his promise.

I knew immediately when we arrived home that the horrible news I'd heard about Godfrey was true. The house was bustling with activity. My uncles' friends, my mother's friends and neighbours were all there, looking shell-shocked and heartbroken. I can't remember where Tshepiso was but I hadn't seen her when I arrived home. Or perhaps I did but I hadn't realise it was her because of the hazy fog that was permeating my head.

That week flew by quickly. I remember very little about it. I made a conscious decision to block it from my memory because it hurt too much to remember. But the story is that my uncle and his best friend, a young man from Zone 9, known only as 'Voetpaitjie', had gone to the Dobsonville Shopping Complex not too far from Meadowlands, armed. Their mission was to disarm the security guards who stood outside the banks, and use their weapons in a heist that they were planning. Unfortunately, the guards had retaliated when Godfrey pointed a pistol at them. Realising they were outnumbered, Voetpaitjie and Godfrey had tried to run away from the complex but were pursued by the armed security guards. The guards had opened fire on the fleeing suspects, wounding both of them. Voetpaitjie had been shot in the foot. My uncle, on the other hand, suffered more severe injuries. Two bullets had lodged themselves in his spinal cord and one in his head. The two were rushed to hospital immediately. Voetpaitjie was arrested as soon as he'd received medical attention. But Godfrey had gone into a coma and never woke up from it.

I didn't cry at all during the week of preparations for my uncle's funeral. I was the only one in the family who didn't cry during that dreadful week. I could not bring myself to mourn even though I knew that it was important for my own healing. But a week later, I locked myself in the toilet outside the house, buried my head between my thighs, and cried my eyes out. I cried for my uncle and the cruelty of his death. I cried for my grandmother, who had lost yet another child. I cried for my family, for the hardness with which Godfrey's death had struck all of us. I cried for Never-never, the magical place I would never see. But above all, I cried for South Africa, because it had lost one of its most amazing sons. That was the first and the last time I ever cried for a dead person. After Godfrey's death, my eyes went dry. I could no longer cry for dead people, no matter how close to me they may have been.

Later, I would understand that there are many Godfreys in this country: young men who have given up on the Rainbow Nation and resorted to a life of crime. We are often made to believe that crime is committed by bad people who have no regard for human life or for peace. This is not true. I don't mean to defend my uncle's actions but crime in the new South Africa is often committed by young men and women who see it as the only ticket out of a life of cruel suffering. When a black child does his best to make an honest living but doors of learning are shut in his face or he is subjected to the cruellest exploitation in the workplace, very little options are left for him. In the 2008 movie *Gangster's Paradise: Jerusalema*, one of the characters, Mbolelo Nazareth, an MK veteran who returns to the country and becomes a criminal mastermind, captures it most aptly when he says, 'Crime is the fastest growing industry in South Africa'.

And this rampant crime is going to claim the lives of more Godfreys and Voetpaitjies: young men who had the misfortune of being born into the black condition.

Last born of the revolution

MY UNCLE'S DEATH LEFT A VOID IN MY HEART. I had loved him with every fibre of my being. We had not been very close in the true sense of the word but he had been my favourite of my three uncles, mainly because he was friendlier to Tshepiso and me. Lesley would resurface but we were to see him only very rarely, and Vina and Ali were often too busy with their own friends to really pay us attention. Not Godfrey. Whenever he was around, he would sit with us and tell us stories about Never-never. He also asked about our schoolwork and life in general. He'd been a good uncle to us.

After Godfrey's death, my family changed completely. My grandmother became paranoid, claiming her son had been killed with muti. She insisted she needed to go and become a sangoma but first she'd have to attend the preparatory school for a year. And so she left the house and went to live where she was being trained to become a sangoma. My mother, who had been closest to Godfrey, was very resigned and often in a very foul mood. After my grandmother left, my mother was left with the responsibility of heading the household. And so, between her busy work schedule and her political activities, she also had to look after her younger siblings and me. The burden was very heavy on her shoulders.

Not long after Godfrey's death, for a reason I never understood, we were evicted from our home in Tlhomedi Street. I have no recollection of the exact day but I recall that a few months after we buried Godfrey, we were back in Sekhwiri Street, this time a few houses away from the shack we had rented years before. We were staying in yet another shack, this one smaller than the last. It was around early 2001, I was ten years old and still in Tshimologo Junior, completing grade 4. Tshepiso had gone to Retlile Senior Primary School. Tshimologo ended with grade 4 so students would transfer to Retlile for their senior primary schooling.

This was the saddest period of my childhood. The humiliation of moving from a proper home back into a dilapidated shack with rusted corrugated iron and holes along the roof edges was more than I could bear. At times, when we had arguments with our friends, they would tease us about living in a shack. It was humiliating. Tshepiso and I began to isolate ourselves from other children, finding comfort in each other. I made new friends, two younger girls called Pepsy and Lerato, who because of her emaciated and tiny frame we called 'Monang', meaning 'mosquito'. I had nothing much in common with them but they were different from my older friends. Perhaps because they were younger they were less judgemental and cruel. I enjoyed their company and often sat with them inside the shack that I called home, in no way embarrassed by its condition. One afternoon, while Monang and I were sitting inside the boiling shack waiting for Pepsy to come so the three of us could go play at the tennis court not too far from home, it began to rain. It poured as if a dam had burst. The leaking roof was split open by the ferocious downpour. The two of us stood inside the flooded shack, watching helplessly as the water seeped into the only sofa in the shack, which was used by Tshepiso as a bed. Utensils and cutlery were floating above the pool of water that had formed inside. The bed, in which my mother slept, was consumed by the water. Everything in the shack was sunk into the pool that was now reaching my knees. As quickly as the rain had started it suddenly stopped, leaving destruction in its wake. Monang and I stood beside each other, our feet drowned, looking helplessly at the debris surrounding us. Pots and pans were strewn about. Suitcases that contained my family's clothes were dripping wet. My school bag was floating above the water, its contents obviously now mashed. It was a heartbreaking experience and for the first time since I had befriended these younger girls, I felt humiliated beyond measure.

Monang and I proceeded to use buckets to get rid of the water inside the shack. The process took hours. Vina and Ali eventually arrived home and lent us a helping hand. After that day, I never hung out with Monang or Pepsy again and, eventually, I returned to our old friends.

———◆———

Although greatly depressed by the new conditions and having to head the household alone because of my grandmother's departure to her sangoma initiation school, my mother's political activism did not falter. By this time, she was actively leading the ANC Youth League (ANCYL) and contributing to the Women's League. She had also found another political home in the form of the South African National Non-Governmental Organisation Coalition (SANGOCO), where she was employed as a communications support officer. SANGOCO was doing developmental work in and around the country. My mom would come home from work to prepare supper for us before heading out to one of her Youth League meetings. More often than not she'd take me with her to these meetings, while Tshepiso preferred to stay home with Ntswaki, from whom she had become inseparable.

By this time, ten years old, I was a regular at your gatherings in Soweto. My mother would always take me with her to meetings and other events around the township. By this time, my father was an undergraduate student at the University of the Witwatersrand, leading the South African Students Congress (SASCO) on campus. When I was not with her at Mapedi Hall in Meadowlands, I was with him in Braamfontein attending meetings of SASCO and the ANC Youth League. I had come to be known as 'the last born of the revolution' in my township and when my mother did not have me in tow to her gatherings, her comrades would ask after me. Not that I did much at these gatherings, hardly anything at all. I'd just sit through the discussions, understanding nothing, and only participate when they started singing revolutionary struggle songs. There was one in particular that I loved and when comrade Clifford Sedibe (I had started calling all members of the ANC 'comrade' by that time) belched it out, I would join in enthusiastically and sing at the top of my lungs:

Comrade MmeMahlangu, Ao botse Solomon
Hore scorpion sena
O na se bona kae.
Comrade MmeMahlangu,
Ao botse Solomon
Hore scorpion sena O na se bona kae.
Thabeng tsa Angola! Thabeng tsa Angola! Tsa Angola
Se ne se ja maBuru!

I didn't understand the message behind this song. I didn't know what a scorpion that killed the Boers was. I did not know what Solomon Mahlangu was doing in the mountains of Angola, or why his mother was being asked where her son got the scorpion that was killing Boers. But I knew that something about this song touched me in very many ways. It was a beautiful song and the look on comrade Clifford's face when he sang it told me that whatever the story behind it was, it was a powerful one. I vowed to myself that someday I'd find out what the story behind this song was and that I too would sing it with the passion that emanated in comrade Clifford's tenor, when I too, like him, would be a leader of the ANC. I would later discover that the song is a dedication to an MK combatant's training in Angola. Nineteen-year-old Mahlangu was hanged by the apartheid police after being convicted of the Goch Street bomb attacks.

The ugly face of the 'Rainbow Nation'

AT THE END OF THE YEAR 2001, my mother informed Tshepiso and me that we would be leaving Tshimologo Junior Primary and Retlile Senior Primary schools respectively and start attending a multiracial school in the northern suburbs of Johannesburg. To say we were thrilled would be putting it mildly. For many years, I'd envied the scores of children in my township who paraded their fancy Model-C school uniforms around the neighbourhood every afternoon. Most of them wore blazers and ties. Even the girls! They all looked so suave and dignified in their uniforms and I always craved the feeling of wearing a uniform just like theirs. Hardly any township school had a uniform that consisted of a blazer and tie. In summer, we wore tunics and shirts. In winter, girls wore knee-length pinafores with long socks or thick wool stockings and long-sleeved jerseys. The boys wore grey pants with shirts.

Upon being informed that we would be taken out of the township schools, I immediately decided to cut my relaxed hair and start dreadlocks. My mother had had them for just over a year by then and was always telling us that dreadlocks are an expression of blackness. I decided that, even as I was leaving the township to study in white suburbs, I would take my identity along with me. I wanted to retain my identity no matter how consuming the multiracial environment was. I had seen many children in the township who had gone to these schools being transformed into what we called 'coconuts': black on the outside and white on the inside. And while I envied their uniforms and sophisticated demeanour, I was appalled by the way they related to those of us who were less privileged than they were. They hardly ever played with us. They did everything in their power to steer clear of us, avoiding us like the plague. And when they did speak to us, once in a blue moon, it would be in English spoken with a twang. It was always a humiliating experience to speak to them because those of us who were studying in the township had a dismal command of the English language and so we'd mumble incoherently, ashamed yet determined to prove to them that we were not inferior, that our education was not inferior.

And so I wanted to enter their world, to be part of their

reality but on my own terms. I wanted to wear their blazers and ties, to travel in their school buses, to look as dignified as they did. But I wanted to do this as Malaika Lesego Samora Mahlatsi, a product of the township, a product of Meadowlands Zone 8. I wanted that part of my identity not to be destroyed.

When I informed my mother that I wanted to have dreadlocks she was thrilled beyond measure. She immediately made an appointment for me with her own hairdresser, abuti Vusi. He agreed that he'd start with my dreadlocks in a week's time. But a week was too long. I was impatient and excited all at the same time. I wanted my hair locked immediately, and so I went to one of the older boys in my neighbourhood, Veli, who also worked at a salon but often rendered services to people from his own home, to start on my hair immediately. Veli agreed and, soon thereafter, he proceeded to cut the relaxed part of my hair off, leaving only the part that had started developing growth. A day after that, he had locked my hair into a terrible mess. Needless to say, my mother was not amused.

When Tshepiso and I informed our friends that we would be transferring to a multiracial school they were genuinely excited for us. The nature of our friendship with Dipuo and Ntswaki in particular was such that none of us could ever feel jealous of another. We loved one another dearly and were as inseparable as a tongue and saliva. It was a happy time after a period of suffocating sadness and despair.

At the beginning of 2002, Tshepiso and I were students at Melpark Primary School in Melville, a beautiful cosmopolitan neighbourhood in the north-west of Johannesburg. Melpark Primary was completely different from Tshimologo. It was a three-storey building with four classrooms on each floor for the senior phase. The junior phase section of the school was separate from where the older students studied. It had its own quad and playground. The reception area was magnificent, with doors that opened out into the quiet street. The offices of the principal, the finance secretary and the admin clerk were situated in the same building. There was a sickroom for boys and a separate one for girls. A staff kitchen and meeting room were also situated in the vicinity. Outside this block was a huge quad area for senior phase students. Directly opposite the quad was a grand hall where weekly assemblies and formal events were held. There was a tuck shop just next to the hall that sold refreshments during breaks. The piano room was located at the other end of the quad, necessarily far from other classes but next to the computer laboratory, which, at that time, had approximately thirty computers: enough for an entire classroom. A lapa was situated behind the quad and would be open during lunch breaks for students who didn't want to sit on the bleachers on the field behind the grand hall. The field had a netball court, a soccer pitch, a softball pitch and athletic tracks. It was a beautiful school, unlike anything I'd ever seen, even on television. As I toured the premises with Tshepiso, we couldn't help but compare it with Tshimologo and Retlile, which had no field, no proper playing grounds, no grand hall for assembly, no piano room and no computer laboratories. It made sense why the children in our neighbourhood who attended this kind of school believed themselves superior to all of us. This privilege they were exposed to was extraordinary and exclusive.

But my first month at the school was a living nightmare. I was in a class with students who'd been there since grade 1. They'd known each other for many years and had developed close friendships, which they guarded jealously. They were grouped with their own circle of friends and it was difficult to be part of any of these circles. My command of the English language was terrible; I could barely speak a complete sentence. But more than that, I looked completely out of place in that class. I was a very dark child with a mane of dreadlocks. This was at a time when little could be done with dreadlocks except to braid them in one style or tie them backwards. The problem with this was that my dreadlocks were not long enough to be tied backwards or braided. So they were just a mane of hair that looked rather untidy. The girls in my class all looked very neat, with their relaxed hair tied into cute buns or plaited precisely. Some even had long braids and synthetic ponytails. The first day I stood in front of my classmates, I was a heap of nerves. Never before had I felt so uncomfortable in my own skin. I felt ugly and was certain that all those children were looking at me like I was a laughable figure of pathos. I was extremely grateful when the bell rang to announce lunch break. I ran out of the classroom to look for Tshepiso and, when I found her, she enveloped me with her fragile arms. She'd gone through the same experience; she understood what I was feeling.

Back in the township, everyone was excitedly asking about our Model-C experience. Ntswaki and Dipuo wanted to know what it felt like to be in the same class with white and Indian students. They wanted to know what it felt like to have white teachers and beautiful classrooms that had no broken chairs or scratched tables. They too, like us before the year 2002, had dreamt of attending multiracial schools where the students wore blazers and ties. It was a dream that many children in the township had. But now Tshepiso and I had finally got the chance to live this dream. And yet it did not bring me the happiness I had anticipated. I felt lost in that world, unable to find the way back to myself. I could not identify with the superficial monotony of my new life. It was suffocating me and I wanted out of it. But I didn't dare to say all this to anyone, least of all my friends. I was terrified that they would tell my mother what I had told them and she in turn would be crushed.

Our being at Melpark Primary School was not a result of a windfall that had happened at home. My mother was still employed at an NGO and was the sole breadwinner in the household, looking after me, Tshepiso, Vina and Ali. We were still living in a shack, the same one that had almost been destroyed by heavy rains a year before. My grandmother was still at her sangoma school. Things were rather difficult and it was becoming increasingly harder for my mother to make ends meet but she was determined to take us out of township schools. She wanted us to have a better chance at escaping the clutches of poverty than she had had, than many children who are confined to township life ever would. And as she would always tell us, 'The ANC fought hard so that you would have these privileges, so that you too would have the opportunities that were only available to white children in the past. I joined the ANC because of this and the two of you shall be beneficiaries of the gains of that struggle.'

I could not tell her that I wanted none of those gains. I could not tell her that the privilege of being in a multiracial school meant little when being in that environment was taxing me emotionally. I was terrified of revealing to her the truth about this new South Africa that she so desperately wanted us to embrace: that in Melpark Primary School, rich black students and white students were treating the rest of us like inferior beings, flashing their wealth before our desperate eyes. And so I kept quiet.

As the weeks went by, Tshepiso and I made new friends and Melpark Primary School, with all its foreign ways, became bearable. But, despite the improvements, I was still battling to feel a sense of belonging. My English had improved and I was doing well academically but something was missing in me, something that I left at the gate every morning when I entered the school premises and only found again when I stepped onto the streets of Meadowlands Zone 8.

Escaping into a
world of books

A YEAR AFTER WE STARTED attending Melpark Primary School, it was decided that Tshepiso and I would begin to take public transport to school. This was done primarily to economise. A Putco bus cost nearly half of what we were paying to be picked up from home.

There were many disadvantages to this new development. Firstly, it meant that we'd have to wake up earlier than before as we had to walk a few kilometres to the bus stop, which was located in Zone 7. The twenty-minute walk was gruelling on winter mornings as it was often very cold and misty when we left home. One of my uncles always accompanied us for protection. In summer, it was equally a nightmare as it would rain. Even with raincoats on, we'd still get a little bit wet. Secondly, Putco buses had a strict schedule. If it happened that we were late, we'd have to wait longer for another bus to arrive and inevitably arrive late for school. The lateness would earn us detention for the day. The detention took place during lunch breaks and so we'd have nothing to eat until second break, by which time we would be ill from hunger. Thirdly, because Putco buses were used mainly by working men and women, they were often full to capacity and we'd have to stand on our feet for the entire hour-long trip from Meadowlands to Melville. At times we'd have seats but would have to give them up for the elderly halfway into the journey. And, for me, the most frustrating thing about using Putco buses was the sermons we were subjected to. For some reason, some pastors felt it necessary to preach in buses and so on some days, mostly Mondays, an old man would conduct a sermon for passengers, complete with prayer and loud preaching. Most passengers enjoyed these sermons, so it would have been futile to lodge a complaint with Putco's management even if we'd wanted to. The only option was to bear the torture quietly.

At school, I continued to work diligently. I joined the netball and softball teams. I wasn't particularly good at netball but I enjoyed playing goalkeeper for the under-13 team. I made the first team for softball, a sport I'd never heard of until I went to Melpark Primary. One of the most unfortunate things about township schools is how few sports and extramural activities are available to students. Most schools in Soweto to this day continue to offer only netball and soccer as sports and choir as a cultural extramural activity. Little else is offered; it's as if the poor black students there are destined to only ever play soccer and netball while those in Model-C schools have a variety of options to choose from, from swimming to piano lessons and chess.

One afternoon while waiting for our netball coach to arrive at the practice site, we were informed that the practice session had been cancelled. Annoyed because I'd missed the bus and would have to wait for over two hours for the next one to arrive, I decided I'd walk around Melville to pass time. I noticed a shop perched at the top of a pharmacy on the main road. It had a big sign that read 'Bounty Hunters Charity Shop'. I immediately crossed the busy street and ascended a flight of stairs to the shop. It was small, made even smaller by huge boxes piled atop each other in every corner and tonnes of books stacked against the walls. There were strange artefacts on the floor and everywhere about the place. It was a complete mess.

I walked slowly around the shop, making sure not to step on anything, hard though that was. A stale odour permeated the atmosphere in the room like a coiling miasma, making me feel claustrophobic. But I was drawn to this shop, to its strange treasures. The only time I'd seen that number of books was at the school's media centre and library, where I only usually went when I was sent to deliver a message to Mrs B, the teacher responsible for its upkeep. Although I had once sat in the media centre during lunch break when I was avoiding other students after an embarrassing incident that had occurred in my first year at Melpark Primary School. My English teacher, Mrs M, who was also my registration teacher, had come to class in tears one morning. All the students were worried and soon gathered around her to comfort her. Being detached from my peers and not necessarily being close to Mrs M, I sat in my chair watching the scene before me with relative interest. After she'd received hugs and kisses from everyone, she eventually gained her composure. She stood at the front of the class and announced to us that she was in a bad emotional state because the previous night her dog had died after being run over by a speeding car in her neighbourhood of Brixton. Everyone looked very sad on her behalf; some even had tears in their eyes. Without thinking, I burst out laughing. It seemed absurd to me that an adult would literally cry because a dog had died. Someone asked me angrily why I was laughing and I replied, 'Who cries over dogs? A dog is not a human being so why would anyone cry when it dies? It's stupid!'

At this, Mrs M stormed out of the class in a fit of rage. Everyone else remained seated, all of them throwing me daggers. I couldn't understand why everyone was looking at me with such anger and resentment in their eyes. It sounded very comical to me that someone who was usually as composed as Mrs M was would be reduced to tears by the death of a mere animal. In Soweto, dogs died all the time but no one ever cried for them. It was unheard of for anyone to have an attachment to a dog so strong that its death would induce sadness in them. Stray dogs littered the neighbourhood, walking through its dusty streets in search of leftover food from bulging trash cans. This was our reality and I had trouble comprehending how other people could have such a strong emotional attachment to dogs.

When she returned to class a few minutes later, Mrs M walked straight to my desk and started barking at me. She claimed I was selfish and heartless, that I was insensitive and undeserving of a place in Melpark Primary School. According to her, the school was a haven for goodhearted people, not mean and disrespectful people like me. Feeling embarrassed by her scolding me in front of my peers, I decided to retaliate. I yelled back at her, telling that she was in no position to tell me I didn't belong there because she was not paying my fees. The exchange went back and forth until I screamed, 'You white people are not normal! Imagine a normal person crying for a useless dog!'

I was kicked out of class on that day. My classmates were angry with me. By the time the bell rang for lunch break, the whole school knew about the incident. Everyone thought I was a bad person and gave me unwelcome stares. Feeling ashamed of myself and terrified of the stares, I opted to spend break alone in the media centre, which was open to students. I didn't read anything. I just sat there looking out into space, replaying the incident over and over again in my head. Needless to say, I couldn't return to class until I apologised publically and privately to Mrs M who, by that time, had recovered from her mourning phase. It was to be the first of many apologies that I would later be forced to make at Melpark Primary School.

Now, as I walked around Bounty Hunters Charity Shop, I

began to read the titles of the many second-hand books that lined the walls and shelves. I was fascinated by them and drawn to the stories they promised to tell as I read through the blurbs. I didn't understand some of the words used but I nonetheless continued to pick up book after book, flipping it right over to read the blurb before putting it back in its place and picking up yet another. This went on for over an hour until I came across a book authored by one David Morrell. The title of the book, *Blood Oath*, didn't sound intriguing but the storyline certainly did. I was overcome by a strong desire to read the entire book. I walked up to the tired-looking cashier and inquired about the price. When she flipped through to the first page of the book to where a price had been scribbled and informed me that the book cost two rand, I nearly jumped out of my skin with excitement. I'd been in the shop for well over an hour reading the blurbs of many books but hadn't bothered to check their prices, which I now discovered were penned at the top of the first page of each book. I returned to the shelf from which I'd picked up *Blood Oath* and begun looking at the prices of the books. The most expensive book there was from an encyclopaedia set and it cost about ten rand!

I had a little money on me saved up from my week's allowance. My mother gave us two rand a day, which she needn't have because we took a balanced packed lunch, including a meal, a bottle of juice, yoghurt, Simba chips and fruit, to school. Because of this I was able to save some money. The books I bought that day would be the first four books I ever read, and they would change my life dramatically. They were *Blood Oath* by David Morrell, *Shall We Tell the*

President? by Jeffrey Archer, *Summer's End* by Danielle Steel and *A Darkness More than Night* by Michael Connelly. They were not revolutionary books. Nothing about them was ideological. They were fiction books about summer romances and psychotic assassins. But they opened me up to a whole new world and introduced me to the power of words. I had entered into a space I immediately knew there was no walking out of, a space that brought me more happiness than I'd ever known. A walk taken out of frustration had led me to my destiny. Books became a part of my life on that day, and today they define a great part of me.

Refusal to assimilate into whiteness

A YEAR AFTER WE TRANSFERRED to Melpark Primary School, my mother decided that Tshepiso and I had to enrol for weekend drama lessons at the Johannesburg Youth Theatre. She was trying very hard to get us off the streets of the township, which had claimed far too many casualties and were breeding grounds for teenage pregnancy, drug use and alcoholism. Tshepiso, who had always got away with more than I ever could, somehow managed to talk my mother out of her own enrolment, leaving me to go through it on my own. And so, in February 2003, I was enrolled for drama and singing lessons at the Johannesburg Youth Theatre in the northern suburb of Parktown, two taxis away from Soweto.

I knew the very first day I walked into the drama class that I would hate every minute of it. There was not a single black face in the room. Not one. It was a sea of strawberry blond and platinum blond. There was long black hair, brunette and even carrot hair. There were all types of hairstyles except an afro or dreadlocks. There were green, blue and grey eyes. There was every race in that room except the black race. It was as if I'd walked into a whole new world, a foreign planet where no black person had ever dared to tread. And I was not only uncomfortable standing in that room, I was resentful. Yes, I was resentful towards all those white and Indian children, not for anything they'd done to me personally but for the vulgar opulence that defined their lives. They were dropped off and picked up by big luxurious cars in the mornings and after classes. They had fancy sandwiches for lunch, food I only ever saw on magazine pages. They wore expensive jewellery and had cellphones. And I, the only black student there, walked from the taxi stop and had polony with cheese for lunch every weekend. I had no fancy cellphone. And yet, back in the township, I was considered privileged! The injustice filled me with resentment and a great anger towards these students and teachers, none of whom was black.

I liked nothing about the Youth Theatre; it represented everything I detested. The elitism of the institution was ten times worse than that of Melpark Primary School. And this time around I didn't hide my feelings from my mother. I went back home one afternoon and told her straight that I would not return to classes the following weekend. My mother, of course, would hear none of it.

She made it clear that not only would I return but I would learn to enjoy it. She accused me of being an ungrateful child who had no sense of appreciation for the hardships she was going through to give me a better life. I lost the debate. I had to return to the Johannesburg Youth Theatre and deal with the boring and snobbish white children who populated my class.

A few months went by without incident. And then, one day, a director of the theatre announced that they would be holding auditions the following weekend for a big play that was coming up. It was called *Sleeping Beauty*. All of us were forced to audition for roles in the play. I didn't put much effort into the preparations for my auditions. I didn't care whether or not I made the list of the main cast. I didn't get any of the leading roles but was cast as a slave in one of the scenes.

Rehearsals were torture. It was clear to everyone on set that I had no desire to be part of the production and I suppose no one was brave enough to demand effort from me. When I think of it in retrospect, I realise they were caught in a catch-22. They didn't want to antagonise me because I was black and, in the new South Africa, white guilt is the cousin of white supremacy. White people are afraid to confront us even on serious matters because they fear that exercising their authority, even necessarily, could be read by us as racism (in most cases it is). On the other hand, they could not take me out of the play because there would be no blacks left in it and this would make them seem racist (again, most of them were). They were all nice to me and, while I wasn't rude, I didn't try too hard to fit in with them. During break time, I would sit alone reading or walk around the vast lawn on the premises, picking up pebbles and throwing them into the air. I had no problem being on my own; in fact, I preferred it that way.

One afternoon, after a morning of running around and practising scenes over and over, I was exhausted. When my scene came up, in which I had to run onto the stage and kneel before the wicked fairy Eva who had poisoned *Sleeping Beauty*, I tripped on the stage. Two of the directors jumped right off their chairs from the viewing gallery and shouted at me. I was extremely upset by this because many others before me had committed mistakes at some point during rehearsals, so I couldn't understand why my mistake provoked such a scolding. I glared at both of them, swore quietly and ran off the stage. They were hot on my heels. I ran to the back of the building, closed myself in an empty room and sat quietly, anger seeping out of every pore in my skin. A few minutes later, the directors ran into the room. One of them had tears streaming from her big blue eyes. She tried to reach out to me but I turned away, my back facing her. In a calm voice, they pleaded with me to go to the office. Hesitantly, I did. There, both of them apologised to me. One, speaking in a muffled voice, explained to me that they were just feeling tired and I'd caught them on a bad day, to which I responded without thinking, 'I am tired too and I am also having a bad day so you have no right to take out your stress on me because I don't take mine out on you!'

That was the second time I'd snapped at a white person. In fact, thinking back, I was never afraid of being vocal about my feelings towards white people. It had to do with my socialisation. For many years in my life I'd been surrounded by men and women who always discussed the painful past. They always discussed the brutality that black people were subjected to under white rule, the brutality of being treated like animals. I grew up going to rallies where songs that spoke about the cruelty of white people were sung. This socialisation left an imprint on my young mind—it taught me to rebel against white authority.

I didn't return to the Johannesburg Youth Theatre after that. I simply told my mother that I would not go there even if she beat me up. When she asked why, I looked her straight in the eyes and without flinching said, 'Because I am sick and tired of acting in plays about white sleeping beauties and singing songs by Westlife. I don't want any part of this. Take me to a community theatre where I can at least act out real stories and sing Brenda Fassie songs. Not this thing of white people.'

She didn't fight with me. She simply looked at me with a tired look in her eyes and said, 'Ok, Lesego.'

My introduction to civil society politics

My final year at Melpark Primary School was a turning point in my life. It was the year 2004 and I was at the peak of my academic excellence. I was elected into the Learners' Representative Council and was the head monitor of the media centre and library. I was also the class captain and in the first team of all the sports I was playing: netball, softball and, by this time, girls' soccer. I was also part of all cultural extramural activities: traditional dancing, school choir, the debating and public-speaking society and the poetry team. My academic record was great. I'd gone from knowing barely any English two years before to being the top English student in the grade. I could write a two-page essay in ninety minutes. English became my favourite subject, followed closely by Natural Science and Human and Social Sciences, the primary school equivalent of History, which would also become one of my favourite subjects in high school. I'd got over the culture shock of Melpark Primary School and begun to embrace it as a part of my life I had to actually be present in.

My mother must have realised the year before that I was finding the transition from the township neither easy nor exciting. After the disastrous experience at the Johannesburg Youth Theatre, she'd enrolled me in dance lessons with a renowned choreographer, Somizi Mhlongo, who I knew from *Sarafina!*, a revolutionary movie about the student uprisings of the 1970s. And so, every Saturday morning, I'd catch a taxi to the Auckland Park campus of Technikon Witwatersrand, where I'd have dance lessons until the afternoon. I was doing ballet, contemporary and tap dancing. The dance lessons boosted my confidence in very many ways. I was the youngest in the class and received the most attention from Somizi and the other students, most of whom were professional dancers. They doted on me. When they looked at me they saw a 'cute and chubby' little girl, not a dark and fat child, which I had long convinced myself was how I was seen by my fellow schoolmates. Sometimes after class Somizi and his partner, Uncle Tom, would take me out with them. They'd take me to McDonald's or to Milky Lane for ice-cream. We often went to visit one of their friends, Sharon Dee, in Northcliff. She too was a known figure, a kwaito star whose hit song, *Local is Lekker*, had at one point been very popular in my township. I was surrounded by great people who cared a lot about me and this helped me to settle better into a world I was battling to adjust to.

Back at home, my grandmother had returned from her sangoma school. Having been let off by Kagiso Trust, she had returned to working in the kitchens, this time for a Jewish family in Dunkeld, an affluent suburb in the north of Johannesburg near Hyde Park. She'd become very resigned and was a shadow of her former self. My uncles had completed their matric and were in tertiary institutions. Ali, the younger of the two, was enrolled with the Federated Union of Black Arts, better known as the FUBA Arts Academy. He was doing a national diploma in Drama and Directing. Vina was enrolled with the South West Gauteng College, studying towards a Mechanical Engineering national diploma. The financial burden had become heavier for my mom but she wanted all of us in school and she was determined to see to it that we had qualifications that would enable us to escape the cycle of poverty that gripped the township.

My mother's activism in the student movement had imprinted itself on her heart. She always told us that she was destined to be an activist her entire life. Because of this, she only ever wanted to work in the civil society sector, where she believed there was a greater chance of making a significant change in the country. When I was completing my final year at Melpark Primary School, she was still employed as a communications support officer at SANGOCO. The SANGOCO offices were in Auckland House in Braamfontein, less than fifteen minutes from Melville. Instead of heading straight home after my dancing practice, I began to take a Metrobus to Braamfontein to wait for her to knock off from work. We would walk down to Bree taxi rank in the central business district and wait in long queues for taxis to Meadowlands. Sometimes at the offices I would just sit and read. Other times, I would play in the elevators, going up and down the building for no reason at all. But, one afternoon, one of my mother's colleagues, abuti Nhlanhla Ndlovu, called me up to his office. I thought he'd scold me for getting up to mischief but instead he gave me a pile of papers and told me to read them. I took them to my mother's desk and began to sort through them one at a time.

The papers were mostly articles, newsletters and pages photocopied from journals about two conferences: the World Summit on Sustainable Development and the World Conference against Racism. I'd heard about these conferences from my mother a few years before. She had not been speaking to me per se—she was probably speaking to one of her many comrades—but I'd heard her make mention of them and, at some point, she'd left home to be in Durban for a few days to attend one of these conferences. I later learned that it was the World Conference against Racism.

I sat in my mom's office looking through the stack of papers until I came across one document in particular that really caught my attention. It was a few pages, no more than ten, stapled together. The cover page read, 'World Children's Prize for the Rights of the Child'.

The document contained stories of children from all across

the world who had been faced with difficult circumstances, such as abuse and discrimination. These children had stood up against the injustices of the system by being activists. The first story was of Xolani Nkosi Johnson, a young South African boy who had fought tirelessly against the discrimination of HIV-positive children. Infected with the incurable disease during his mother's pregnancy, Nkosi had been adopted by a white woman named Gail Johnson, who had been instrumental in Nkosi's journey and battle with the dreaded disease. A hospice for mothers and children living with the disease, Nkosi's Haven, had been established after Nkosi's death in 2001, on World Children's Day. I knew Nkosi Johnson's story. He had been a student at Melpark Primary School during his death. Teachers always made a point of telling us about him.

But the story that particularly caught my attention on that day was that of Iqbal Masih. I have never forgotten his story.

Iqbal Masih was a young boy from Pakistan who had been forced into bonded labour when he was only four years old by his family, who had borrowed money from a businessman who owned a carpet factory. This system, where a child is forced to pay off a loan that his or her family gets from a businessman, is known as peshgi. The child is not consulted but is just sent to live and slave in a factory as a way of paying off the loan. Over the years, Iqbal's family borrowed more money from the businessman, resulting in Iqbal remaining in the carpet factory for many years. The conditions in the factory were horrific. The children, some as young as three years old, were forced to work fifteen-hour shifts six times a week. They barely had anything to eat. While working, weaving threads into carpets, they weren't allowed to speak to one another. If they dared to, they were beaten to a pulp. At times they'd be hung upside down or placed in solitary confinement.

After having worked for six years in the carpet factory, Iqbal heard about the Bonded Labour Liberation Front (BLLF), an organisation that was working to abolish child labour, which the Pakistani government had outlawed in 1992. Iqbal sought the help of Ehsan Khan, the president of the BLLF, who sent documentation to the businessman that Iqbal worked for. This documentation was evidence that peshgi had been outlawed by the state and erased the debt owed by families to businesses that used child labour as payment for the loans. Iqbal was subsequently set free. Not content with his own freedom while other children were still kept in factories across Pakistan, Iqbal joined the BLLF and began advocating for the liberation of other child slaves in Pakistan and the rest of the world. As a result of his efforts, thousands of children were freed.

Iqbal's popularity grew instantly. His influence caused him to receive death threats, possibly from the businessmen he was freeing child labourers from. On 16 April 1995, aged just twelve, Iqbal was shot and killed while riding a bike on his way to visit an uncle. The details of his death remain a mystery. What is for sure is that twelve-year-old Iqbal Masih became a martyr for a just cause, one of the youngest activists the world had ever seen. After reading the story of this young boy, I read all the other documents that abuti Nhlanhla had given to me.

Along with Bounty Hunters Charity Shop, the SANGOCO offices had become my sanctuary, my own personal library. Iqbal Masih's story had awoken something in me. I wanted to know more, to understand the world of social justice and activism. Years later, I would marry myself to this world.

Parting ways with the Congress Movement

AROUND THE TIME THAT I WAS BEGINNING my initiation into civil society politics, my mother was slowly becoming dejected by the politics of the Congress Movement. We were no longer attending your meetings with the same frequency that we used to in the past. Once in a blue moon, we would go to Mapedi Hall in Meadowlands Zone 2 for a Youth League event. My mom had ceased to be active in the Youth League and was focusing her energies on the work that she was doing with SANGOCO and the other NGOs that she was working with as a volunteer.

I started to notice my mother's unhappiness with you one afternoon just before campaigning for the 2004 general elections started. Usually excited about doing your campaigns, my mother was rather miserable at this period. She would just sit at home reading novels while her comrades were busy conducting door-to-door campaigns in and around the neighbourhood. When I asked her why she was no longer attending your events or helping her comrades to campaign and ensure an ANC victory, she responded that she was tired of you and felt that you were taking the poor for granted.

'How so?' I asked.

She replied that you were not prioritising critical questions that should have been made top priorities immediately after coming into power. These critical matters, she argued, were education and land. According to her, you were making grounds fertile for the creation of a welfare state by not making education your chief project. She was certain that within a decade the country would be plunged into a crisis of great proportions due to your blunders in the education system.

I didn't understand half of what she was saying. As far as I could tell, there was no crisis in the education system save for the infrastructure contrast between township schools and former Model-C ones. I continued to hold the view that the difference was only in what they looked like and some activities they offered, and that the actual quality of education didn't differ much. Tshimologo Junior Primary was just as good a school as Melpark Primary. Its teachers were just as passionate about teaching and the students were just as enthusiastic about learning. I presented this argument to her, telling her that the only crisis was that some schools had better facilities than others. My mother, in a very resigned voice, informed me that the contrast in facilities was not the biggest problem, though it was part of it because without proper facilities schools cannot function to the best of their potential. She argued that in township schools, students could barely use computers and so were destined to be incompetent in the workplace, where computers are a way of life. She argued that a lack of proper laboratories meant that students studying Biology and Physical Science in township schools wouldn't understand some lab-dependent experiments and, as a result, their knowledge and understanding would be compromised. She argued many things about what a lack of proper infrastructure meant for township schools, which were dominated by black students. But this was not the heart of her view that our education was in a state of crisis. The crisis, she argued, arose from the curriculum itself. My mother felt that it was not producing critical thinkers or anything fundamentally different to what the previous system was producing: students who would graduate and serve the unequal system rather than change it.

She also argued that the land question was not being addressed with the enthusiasm that it was addressed during the days of the liberation struggle. With a haunted look, she said to me, 'The ANC has forgotten about the land, Lesego, and yet that is primarily why we were in the struggle in the first place . . .'

She went on to argue that instead of returning land to

the hands of the people you were instead more focused on building them Reconstruction and Development Programme (RDP) houses.

'In the next 20 years, we are going to have more blacks in RDP houses and more whites on farms because of our focus on building more RDP houses and the lack of interest in reclaiming those stolen farms.'

My arguments with her on these topics went on for many months. Every day, my mother would return home from work and tell me stories of injustice happening in some part of the country. She would link these injustices to something that you had done or failed to do. It was a depressing period. I could barely understand half of what she was saying. I had grown up in a community that worshipped you. I was raised in a family of ANC activists and supporters and, suddenly, I was being told that the same ANC was at times the root of problems rather than the solution.

By the time I graduated from primary school in 2004, my mother was no longer a member of the ANC or any structure within the Mass Democratic Movement. She had decided not to renew her membership and was now a fulltime social justice activist working in SANGOCO and community-based organisations. She had lost faith in you. I always believed that she would return, so strong had her love for you been. But she never did. Not the next year or decade. My mother had parted ways with an organisation that she had once lived for.

The strength we drew from the humiliation of poverty

As you are aware, the South African school calendar begins in January. However, I was only placed in school in February 2005 because my mother didn't have money to pay for my registration at Roosevelt High School, where Tshepiso had been enrolled the previous year. And so we had looked around for available options. Most schools were full and the Department of Education had to be called in to intervene. Eventually, I was registered at Florida Park High School, a multiracial school in a former Afrikaans neighbourhood in the west of Johannesburg. While I was disappointed that I couldn't go to Roosevelt High, I was grateful I was in a school that had proper facilities and a good infrastructure, which was a far cry from the schools in Soweto that the Department of Education had also recommended as options due to their close proximity to my home. By this time I had got over the nostalgia of township schools. I had come to the realisation that, indeed, the infrastructural deficiencies in township schools were a serious threat to quality education. And I wanted a quality education because I had decided in my last year of primary school that I wanted to go to university to study law. The reason for this was that I wanted to be president of the Republic of South Africa and I thought that since many politicians had studied law, it would serve me well to study it too. Maybe that way, my chances of occupying the presidential seat would be increased.

Florida Park High School introduced me to myself in more ways than I can ever explain. In grade 10, we were allowed to choose our own subjects. The first subject I chose was Setswana as my first additional language as an alternative to Afrikaans. Throughout high school, I'd hated Afrikaans with a passion. It reminded me of the many stories that my mother used to tell me about her childhood and how the Boers would harass folk in the townships. I hated it because it reminded me of everything I didn't want to think about. And I hated the arrogance of Afrikaans teachers, who treated the subject like it was the most superior in the country.

During my high school life, my family moved thrice. The first move happened in 2006, when I was in grade 9. My grandmother had been given an RDP house by one of her relatives, who had been bought a bigger house in Dobsonville by her children. So we had relocated from our small shack in Zone 8 to Phase 2 in Braamfischerville. I hated everything about our new neighbourhood. In 2006, Braamfischer, as it is called, was not as developed as it is today. Electricity in the area was scarce; we often relied on our paraffin stove for cooking and warming the house. There were hardly any tarred roads and the dust in the area was unbearable. This was worse in autumn when violent winds would rip through the streets, sending waves of dirty particles and sand inside homes. Braamfischer was also far from civilisation. There was no hospital or clinic in the area. The nearest one was Clinix Tshepo-Themba in Meadowlands Extension 11. The problem was that Tshepo-Themba is a private hospital and so none of us could ever have afforded it anyway. The nearest police station was in Dobsonville, as were the nearest schools and shopping complex. There was literally nothing in Braamfischer except small RDP houses where the poorest of the poor lived.

Braamfischer gave a face to the injustice of post-apartheid South Africa. It introduced me to the cruel reality of a divided society that had black people on the receiving end of the brutality. Thousands of families lived below the poverty line in Braamfischer, most of them barely able to afford even mere basics. Every morning as I queued up for taxis to Florida, I would see very small children carrying heavy backpacks, their emaciated bodies being blown around by the angry winds that ravaged the neighbourhood. The uniforms they wore indicated that they studied in schools as far away as Meadowlands Zone 1, a trip that took nearly two hours.

People who had lived in squatter camps and older people were being made a priority by the government so the area was full of people who were unemployed and others who didn't have adequate income. This made the level of crime in the neighbourhood very high. The area was notorious for housebreakings and robberies. Fed up with the crime, the people of Braamfischerville started taking the law into their own hands. Criminals would be subjected to the most brutal mob justice punishments, at times even being necklaced.

I witnessed such an incident one late afternoon when I was coming home from the Florida Community Library, a place I'd made my second home. My house was situated near an open field that was used as a soccer pitch by the boys in the neighbourhood. The open field was near a patch of a bushveld that was used by criminals as a hiding spot due to its vast expanse and strategic location near these grounds, which led directly to the other side of Phase 2. As I walked past the open field on my way home, tired beyond measure, my attention was caught by a loud noise coming from the opposite end of the open field. As I inched closer to inspect the source of the noise, I realised that a group of people were surrounding what looked like a corpse. Terrified, I went to join the group and asked someone standing beside me what had happened.

'Bamo thuntse a utswa ko ntlung ya batho,' was the reply.

The man on the ground looked very young, perhaps in his very early twenties. He was bleeding profusely from a gaping wound on his head. A bloody brick lay beside him, next to an old car tyre. But he wasn't dead. Faint murmurs were coming from his bleeding mouth, his torn lips bruised. He could barely open his eyes because they were both swollen from the beating he'd received from the angry mob. Someone was busy kicking him in the lower abdomen while everyone else stood aside, doing nothing. As I stood there waiting to see what would happen to him, an older man who lived near my house came running with a gallon of petrol. It was only then that I realised what was happening. I'd only ever seen something like this in movies and documentaries about the apartheid era. I never could have imagined it would happen right before my eyes. The infuriated and irrational mob was waiting for the petrol so they could burn this young man. I was terrified beyond measure and I knew I couldn't watch what was about to happen. I knew that the police wouldn't arrive any time soon because there was no police station in Phase 2 at that time. If any had been called, they would have had to come from Dobsonville, which was about thirty minutes away because of the bad roads in Braamfischerville. It was inevitable that the young man would be necklaced, burnt beyond recognition. I quickly ran home, trying with all my might to block out the scene I had witnessed a few minutes earlier.

Later than night, I was informed by Ali that the young man had been killed by the community. He'd been necklaced right there in the open field. Young people had witnessed this, some barely teenagers, and no one had tried to stop this senseless killing. When I raised this with Ali, he responded in a very defeated voice, 'Lesego, I don't agree with the killing. I wish there was another solution. But you must understand that in Braamfischer, solutions are very limited. People here are very poor, they have nothing. They're just trying to survive with the little they have. These criminals break into homes and steal from these people. There are no police officers anywhere to help. Even when the police are called, they take hours to arrive. Sometimes they don't even come at all. What would have happened if there had been a little girl in the house when the criminal entered? He would have raped her, maybe even killed her. What are people supposed to do in this situation? What were they supposed to do?'

I didn't understand this explanation. I knew that he was making a valid point but I didn't believe that there truly was no solution to the problem. To accept that explanation would have been to reconcile myself to the inevitability of another necklacing in the not-so-distant future. I did not want to believe that more than a decade into the new dispensation, necklacings could be normal in South Africa. I could understand why impimpis during the apartheid era deserved to be necklaced. They were betraying the revolution and compromising the liberation struggle of our people. But in this new South Africa, where there was a promise of a different reality, why was it necessary to burn people alive? There had to be another way. We could not have defeated white domination only to find ourselves killing each other for food! I went to bed with a heavy heart that night.

Incidents of this nature continued to happen in Braamfischer until, eventually, a small satellite police station was built and street committees were established. They were responsible for protecting the community by patrolling at peak hours looking for robberies, mainly in the early mornings and late evenings. A new system was also introduced. Every household was forced to have a whistle, which would be blown when an intruder attempted to enter the house. The repeated blowing of the whistle would alert the community that someone was in trouble. Everyone would then blow their whistles to inform the rest of the neighbourhood and help would come in the form of the people. The criminal would then be immobilised through a non-fatal beating. The police would be called and the suspect incarcerated. The introduction of this system saw a dramatic decrease in criminal activity in the neighbourhood. The people had won the war against crime. Above all, someone's son, someone's brother, was not going to have to watch his own flesh peeling as petroleum penetrated his pores.

——◦•◦——

We lived in Braamfischer for three years. In July 2007, my mother took my younger brother Lumumba, who had been born in 2003, and me out of the neighbourhood. A few months before that, a feud had divided the family irreparably. In the midst of it all, my mother had taken Lumumba, Tshepiso and me to the house of close friends, Mark Weinberg and Celeste Fortuin, to escape the nightmare that was happening in the family. Because of its depth and the wound it inflicted on my family, I have lived my life attempting to bury it, to never have to talk about it with anyone. Perhaps it is the desire to erase it from my consciousness. Maybe one day I will be able to talk about it but I am not quite ready yet.

Mark and Celeste had gone to Cape Town, where they had another house, and left the one in Norwood under my mother's care for a few weeks. The house was not glamorous but it was very big and very comfortable. For a few weeks, the four of us allowed ourselves to forget about everything that was going wrong at home and just focus on being happy. And, indeed, we were very happy.

I used to wake up every morning to listen to one particular song: *I Have a Dream* by Westlife. The Johannesburg Youth Theatre had made me resent anything artistic that didn't relate to my black reality but at that point in my life, Westlife's music became a medicine, healing the brokenness of my soul. I'd sweep and scrub the kitchen floor singing it loudly at the top of my voice.

The day we had to return home was a very painful one. None of us wanted to leave Norwood, least of all me. I had had a taste of what peace feels like and I wanted it. I wanted to take long walks around the quiet streets of Norwood, where old men and women jogged in their skimpy outfits. I wanted to return to a home where there was no shouting and no fighting. I wanted to see my mother laughing and playing with us, where everything was okay. I wanted what didn't exist in Braamfischer, where World War III had been declared within the Mahlatsi family. But Norwood was not our life. It had merely been a temporary haven, a sanctuary where we'd gone to gather the strength necessary to survive the turbulence of life back home.

Soon after we returned from our vacation in Norwood, things got worse at home. It became clear that there would be no reconciliation in the family. My mother decided to take me and my brother and move. We moved to a rented house in Meadowlands Zone 3, a street away from where my mother had grown up. At the time, she was unemployed. After leaving SANGOCO she'd had stints at the Gender & Trade Network in Africa and Southern Africa Communications for Development before moving on to Sidewalk Productions. The struggling production house had few resources to sustain staff on a long-term basis and, as a result, she had leave.

Our move to Zone 3 was a very difficult one. My mom had no

job. Zone 3 was further from my school than Braamfischer had been. Where I had taken one taxi to school in Braamfischer, I was now forced to take two taxis as none went from Meadowlands to Florida directly. Lumumba was also forced to drop out of his multiracial crèche in Creswell Park. It would have been very expensive to keep him there as the fees were high and he would have needed transportation to fetch him from Zone 3. He was enrolled in a local crèche in our new neighbourhood, a far cry from what he'd been used to.

Zone 3 brought me closer to my mother. We were on our own and we needed to be strong for each other and for Lumumba, who was too young to understand what was happening. There was hardly any money at home. Whatever little my mother and I were able to earn would be used to buy clothes and food for Lumumba because we didn't want him to feel the poverty that the family was going through. We wanted him to have what other children had, to not be made to feel inferior in any way.

Because my mother hardly had any money to pay for my fees or my transport to school, I had to learn to make money. I started two businesses at school. The first was selling assignments and essays to students. The business was a very lucrative one because it addressed a basic need for students: passing. I knew it wasn't right, but students didn't want to do their own work but they wanted to pass. They also had a lot of money, which I didn't have. So I began to supply what they demanded and, in the process, made enough money to help out my family with buying groceries and other necessities in the household. I had learned to master the art of writing essays over the years and it was easy for me. I had an excellent command of the English language as a result of my extensive reading, a hobby I'd picked up in Melpark Primary School and at the SANGOCO offices years before, and had never abandoned.

My business grew very quickly. By grade 10, I was writing essays for students in my grade as well as those in grade 11 and matric. I was making hundreds of rands a month, enough money to pay for my own transport and to help out at home. To subsidise this income, I opened another lucrative business: selling sweets at school. I hired my three best friends, Nompumelelo 'Mpumi' Motaung, Palesa 'Worm' Moroe and Kgothatso 'SL' Mudau, to help me with the running of the businesses. Kgothatso was very good with figures so I employed her to manage the finances. Mpumi was a very pretty girl, very popular with students for her looks and sweet demeanour, so she was tasked with marketing both businesses. Palesa, because of her good command of language, would often help me with the writing of assignments and essays. We were making a lot of money. Sometimes we'd blow the money on things like movies and lunches. This would set us back but we always managed to make more money. Even though most of my money went to helping my mother, there were days when I just wanted to be like an ordinary child, to have no worry in the world. I wanted to be able to just blow R200 at the movies at Westgate Mall, or buy one of the Karrimor schoolbags that were so popular with students. I needed, just once in a blue moon, to escape from the burden of being a breadwinner at sixteen years old.

When we were unable to make enough money on time, my best friends would put together money from their own pockets and give it to me for transport. On these days, I'd be unable to help out at home and we'd rely on a feeding scheme known in the townships as 'malebese', which poor people received from the government. My mother would walk to Zone 1 with a two-litre bottle to receive sweetened milk and a loaf of bread with peanut butter and jam. We'd have malebese for breakfast, lunch and supper. If we could spare a few rand, my mother would buy chicken drumsticks for Lumumba. It was the cheapest meat, and the only meat we could afford.

A few months later, my mother, desperate for employment, joined the corporate sector as a personal assistant to a managing director. She was also a client service coordinator and junior copywriter for a below-the-line advertising agency. The following year, we moved to Dobsonville Extension 2, a lower middle-class neighbourhood not too far from Meadowlands. Dobsonville Extension 2 had been established in the late 1980s as a sanctuary for the emerging black middle class. Because of this, there are many professionals, such as doctors, nurses, teachers and businesspeople, in the neighbourhood. Ours was a beautiful peach-coloured house on a cul-de-sac. It had a very small garden where bright flowers were planted. The green grass was a striking contrast to the black-and-red paving on the ground. The yard was not necessarily very big but it had adequate space for a family of three. For the first time in my life I had my own bedroom that I shared with absolutely no one else. My mother also had her own bedroom and so too did Lumumba. All the rooms besides Lumumba's were fitted with built-in wardrobes. There was an indoor toilet that was separate from the bathroom and a small kitchen and lounge. It would be the place I called home for the longest time.

Dobsonville Extension 2 was very different to where I had come from. Because it was associated with the black township middle class it was less rowdy than neighbourhoods like Braamfischerville or the old Meadowlands where I had grown up. People in this township kept to themselves most of the time and there were very few young people out on the streets playing. My grandmother would have said that the people of Extension 2 'bashapa dithupa'.

While I knew my mother hated the private sector, I also knew she hated poverty even more. She hated being unable to put a meal on the table for my little brother and me. She hated having to rely on me to make ends meet in the house and, many times, she told me that it made her feel inadequate as a parent to have a sixteen-year-old bringing home the bacon. When my mother was working at the ad agency, things had improved at home. Lumumba was sent to a multiracial crèche in Roodepoort and also started taking karate lessons in Melville, just as I had taken dance and drama lessons many years before. I had money for transport to and from school every day and my daily allowance was even increased from five to fifteen rand, which at that time was still quite a lot of money for someone who took lunch to school anyway. After many years of struggling, things were looking up.

But the work depressed my mother greatly. She'd worked in the civil society sector her entire life and knew very little about the private sector. She complained about everything: the dress code expected of a corporate employee, the 'cold' environment of the office and above all, the lack of transformation in the advertising sector. My mother always spoke about how, over a decade into a democratic dispensation, there were hardly any black-owned advertising agencies in the country and how the industry is monopolised by a white elite minority.

Your democracy is just a word when even healthcare is a commodity

THE YEAR 2009 WAS MY FINAL YEAR of high school and one of the most difficult years of my life. In October 2008, while writing my final grade 11 exams, my mother fell gravely ill. She woke up one morning and did what she did every morning: took a bath and helped my brother get ready for crèche. After that, she informed me she wasn't feeling too well and would need to go to the clinic to get a prescription for the piercing headaches she said were making falling asleep impossible. We said goodbye to each other, not knowing that it would be almost two months before we'd see one another again.

I returned home from school that afternoon to find my little brother had gone to my grandmother's house in Braamfischer. This puzzled me because it was a weekday and Lumumba had to be in crèche the following day. My mother was very strict about my brother's attendance at crèche because she felt that he had missed out on many things when we sent him to the day care centre in Meadowlands Zone 3, where hardly any education took place. I knew then that something was wrong and feared that we were on the brink of being forced out of yet another house. The memories of what had happened in Tlhomedi just after Godfrey's death came flooding back and I was terrified.

Later that evening, I received a call from my grandmother informing me that my mom was very ill and had been admitted to Parklane Clinic in Parktown, the same clinic where my brother had been born five years before. I was a little worried that she'd been admitted but was not necessarily too alarmed because I'd seen her that morning and she hadn't looked like someone who was deathly ill. My grandmother suggested I come and stay with the family until such time as my mother returned home but I refused her offer. I was fine at home alone; I didn't want to return to my family home where so much had happened, where there were still gaping wounds.

When two weeks passed without my mother returning home I began to panic. I had not heard from her since she'd been admitted. The only thing that kept me sane was the fact that I was writing my final exams and needed to devote my full attention to studying because my results would be used for applying to university. By then I had decided that I wanted to study towards a Bachelor of Science degree, with majors in Nuclear Physics and Environmental Science. I wanted to go to Stellenbosch University and the requirements were strict. I had to perform very well if I wanted a place at the university. I also knew that even with the reasonable salary that she was earning at the ad agency, my mother would not be able to afford my tuition fees and accommodation at the institution, so I had to apply for a scholarship and I had to get it.

For three weeks, I tried to concentrate on my schoolwork and block out everything else but eventually I couldn't do it anymore. There was hardly any food in the house and I had heard no news about my mother's health. I decided to call my grandmother to ask her for details of where my mother was being kept so I could visit her the following day. My grandmother informed me that my mother had asked that I not be allowed to visit her in hospital; she didn't want me to see her in the kind of state that she was in. My grandmother promised to come the following day and she did, bringing with her some basic groceries and money for me to be able to go to school. Because it was exam time, I didn't have to be in school every day and I didn't need a lot of money for transport.

My grandmother informed me that my mother had been admitted to a psychiatric ward because she was suffering from severe depression and unless she received medical help immediately she'd never be able to function as a normal person again. She could even die. The news left me completely devastated. My mother and I had our differences and as I grew older we were beginning to fight all the time. But I loved her dearly and the thought of losing her traumatised me. I did not cry or alert my grandmother that I was falling apart. I continued with the motions of being alive and by the time the year ended, I made it onto the Academic Honours top ten list and managed to score a good number of distinctions.

Two months after she had been admitted to hospital, my mother returned home. By that time, I had conditioned myself to expect the worst. I was euphoric when I returned home from a friend's house to find my mother sitting on the edge of her bed with a newspaper in her hands. And for the first time since I'd stopped going to church more than three years before, I uttered the words, 'Thank you, God!'

My mother informed me that she'd started feeling sick a few months before she was admitted to hospital. She would wake up in the middle of the night with the mother of all headaches, unable to move or even call out for help. She said she'd also been afraid of telling me because she didn't want to worry me so close to my important exams.

Because of the financial implications of being in an expensive hospital, she had stayed in Parklane Clinic for just over a week before being moved to Rand Clinic, where she was placed in a psychiatric ward because of the severity of her mental and emotional deterioration. There, she had been heavily medicated and kept under the watchful eyes of nurses and numerous doctors. As the days went by, she had become so sick that she could no longer even feed herself. My grandmother had visited her daily to assist with bathing and feeding her. She told me that it was a horrendous experience that she would not wish upon her worst enemy.

When she returned home, my mother didn't have a job. She had been fired for failing to report to work, despite the evidence that she had been hospitalised. A staunch activist, she decided to take the company to court for unfair dismissal. But a giant corporation was not going to allow a former employee to humiliate it in public. The company fought back hard and in the end, exhausted and rendered broke by the legal battle, my mother decided to drop the case. This was a very difficult decision for her because she had continued to believe in the principle of her fight right until the end. She believed that she had been hard done by the company, dismissed not only because she had been ill but because she had not fit into the corporate world to begin with. Her radical views, influenced by her lifelong work in the NGO sector, had not been suitable for an environment that was not pro-poor. Her illness had been just what was needed to get rid of her. Broke and dejected, she vowed she would never join the private sector ever again.

She never did. And I never forgave you, ANC, for allowing big business to have a monopoly on legal power in our country. The justice system, like the economic system in our country, is unjust. Laws continue to protect the haves while the have-nots are on the receiving end of exploitation and outright abuse. My mother didn't lose the case because she didn't have a case, she lost it because in a country asphyxiated by structural inequalities and a judiciary that remains untransformed, blacks will never engage in this battle on an equal footing with their rich white counterparts. And that is the reality of democratic South Africa: injustice has a face, and that face is working class, poor and black.

A thousand broken pieces

THINGS BECAME DIFFICULT YET AGAIN when my mother lost her job. But by then, we had grown so used to poverty that it did not send us into a deep state of depression. I was completing my final year at Florida Park High School, where I was still on the Academic Honours roll and had been elected into the Representative Council of Learners (RCL) and Disciplinary Committee. I joined the Debating Society for a brief period before having a major fight with the debating coach, Mrs E, a racist white teacher who had an exaggerated sense of importance. She hated the fact that I refused to polish my views on any political question. This made her believe I was 'pompous'. Our relationship soured to the point where we couldn't work together and I made the conscious decision to leave her society. I didn't need her and I certainly had no desire to subject myself to the shallow topics she liked to pick for debate. Typical of liberals, she shied away from real debates and opted for tame ones that didn't demand too much critical thinking. It was easier for her to have us debate whether euthanasia should be legalised or about the relationship between rap music and teen violence—things I have come to regard as first world problems—than it was for her to have us debating about the race question or property relations in South Africa. I was getting tired of the whole affair.

My matric year was difficult. The last few years were taking their toll on me both academically and emotionally. A few months into the year, I was demoted from the RCL and Disciplinary Committee after I put the school into disrepute by smoking dagga mixed with what I now think may have been benzene, although I didn't know it at the time. I had smoked dagga before but because this time around it had been made impure with other substances, it created a serious imbalance in my body. After a large overdose of the substance, I walked into my first class of the day, Life Sciences, feeling nauseous and out of sorts. Suddenly I woke up that night at Helen Joseph Hospital with a drip attached to my right arm and an absolutely terrible headache. My close friend, Thato Tshabalala, who was standing beside me at the hospital, explained that I had injured myself badly. I'd broken the window of my Life Sciences class and cut my hand open.

Some teachers had tried to restrain me but I'd fought all of them off and injured one, Mrs G, whom I had apparently kicked in the lower abdomen. The tragedy in all this was that Mrs G was one of my favourite teachers. I was dismayed. When I eventually returned to school a few days later, I had to field questions from curious students and angry teachers. Rumour had it that I had had a 'demon attack'. Some people claimed I'd overdosed on crystal meth, a dangerous and highly addictive drug that I'd once been rumoured to have been taking due to my high energy levels.

The school didn't hesitate to haul me before a disciplinary committee and I was demoted from the RCL with immediate effect. I was asked to remove the colourful and prestigious ribbons from my blazer. I was stripped of the privilege to even have my Academic Colours and scrolls on my blazer. Everything I'd worked for was taken away from me and everyone who had once believed in me looked at me with disgust and disappointment in their eyes. I was in a steady relationship with the head boy, Daniel Phiri, who, like I'd been at one point, was an outstanding academic achiever. My demotion affected him badly and our relationship hit a rough patch. But, like a dedicated soldier, he never left my side even when everyone around us, including our teachers, was advising him to do so.

I was performing awfully in most of my subjects, including History and Physical Science, which I had breezed through in previous years. I went from being an A student to being a student who struggled with almost everything. In the first term of matric, I managed to make it into the top five at number three. In the second term, I dropped to number seven and in the third term, I didn't even make the top twenty in the grade. History, for which I'd previously averaged over 90 per cent, plummeted to a shocking 50 per cent. I didn't write four prelim exam papers because there had been no money for me to go to school on the days I was writing the papers and I was at a point where I didn't even care enough to want to make a plan, let alone to tell my best friends about the situation. Because it was exam time, I also couldn't make any money from selling assignments or sweets. I failed Mathematics, Physical Science and Life Sciences. I scraped through History and Life Orientation, the easiest subjects I took, with 50 per cent. The only subjects I did well in were the languages, English and Setswana, which I passed with 89 per cent and 84 per cent respectively.

All my teachers were panicking. No one had any idea what my problem was. I had no idea myself. We were all spectators of Malaika's demise and none of us knew what to do. Eventually, I had to make the very difficult decision to go back to therapy. I'd been in therapy for many years but had thought I would be fine without it. Therapy was still a very foreign concept to black people. I had been uncomfortable going to a therapist to begin with and now, as an older teenager, I felt more resentful about the idea of sitting on a couch talking about my problems. Everyone had problems. Merely by being born black in this country you had problems. I didn't think I'd need therapy to cope with my own circumstances.

I had miscalculated. The vice principal of my school got hold of my former therapist, Dr A, a senior lecturer of Psychology at the University of the Witwatersrand, and arranged an urgent appointment for me. A few days later, I was driven to Braamfontein by one of the school's drivers, Bab'Vee, to see Dr A. Climbing the stairs and walking through the corridors of the Umthombo Building, I could feel my composure falling apart. I could no longer hold myself together. I walked into Dr A's office and fell right into her arms and, for the first time in many years, I cried. I cried for the many times I'd had to be strong. I cried for my mother, who was struggling to make ends meet. I cried for the many times the landlord had almost evicted us from the house that we called home. I cried for my family, which had fallen apart. I cried for the many sacrifices I had been forced to make just to survive. I cried for Lumumba, who I could not shield from the cruel humiliation of poverty. I cried for myself: my dismal academic performance, my demotion from the RCL and Disciplinary Committee and, above all, my inability to be strong. I had been so strong for so long and now I was helpless, weak and vulnerable. Now I was sitting in my therapist's office with a monsoon of tears flooding out of my eyes, unable even to speak. I cried for my naivety, for allowing myself to believe that there is a Rainbow Nation where young people would not have to suffer. I knew then that it was a myth. Young people suffered. Young people did not sleep at night because they had to write assignments to sell so that they could put a meal on the table. Young people had to hustle for money to be able to go to school. Young people were not free, they were chained to a hopeless reality of humiliating poverty and an unbearable heaviness of being.

Hours later, I walked out of Dr A's office without any answers but with a clearer perspective about what was wrong with me. Dr A told me that I had bottled up my pain and buried my traumatic experiences for a long time. I was now unable to continue to be strong and unaffected by everything that had happened in my personal life.

'You need to stop trying to be strong, Malaika. You are only seventeen years old. No child your age should have to be this strong. You are allowed to hurt. You *must* let out all the pain and the hurt that is eating you alive, because if you don't, you could end up in hospital like your mom, diagnosed with depression. And you might not be as lucky as she was: to come out alive . . .'

A part of me agreed with Dr A but another part could not accept that I, Malaika, a township child, could be depressed. What I had to face was what many other children in the township faced. I felt that I had no right to want an easier life than they had.

I continued to see Dr A from that point and tried very hard to get back into form with my academic work. Daniel created a study schedule that he forced me into. I had gone through the year in a daze and, as a result, I was clueless about even the most basic of things, particularly in Mathematics, Physical Science and Life Sciences. I had also opted to do Additional Mathematics, which was done by only a dozen other students at the school. I had applied for a BSc in Physics at Stellenbosch University and got provisional acceptance—I had applied using my grade 11 final results—which would only be finalised once the institution received my matric results. It was almost exam time and I knew barely anything. With his loving kindness, Daniel pushed me to catch up. Our other friends, Diana Mabunda and her boyfriend Kabelo Mautlwe, also played a part by giving me notes for subjects that I didn't have in common with Daniel. We studied intensely.

All three of them lived in the suburbs. Daniel lived in Florida Park, a few minutes from the school, Diana lived in Ruimsig on the west rand and Kabelo lived in Melville. So when I couldn't study with them, I was assisted by my other friends who lived closer to home. Palesa, Mpumi and Kgothatso, my partners in crime, lent a helping hand without complaint. They all wanted me to do well because they all believed in my abilities.

Even though my academic performance was improving, I was stunned when, in late August, I received an invitation to attend the Annual Honours Evening. The ceremony honoured students who had performed exceptionally well throughout the year. I had been attending Honours, as we called it, since my first year of high school. But I didn't in my wildest dreams imagine that in 2009 I would have made it onto the prestigious list. I had not just underperformed, I had *failed* my preliminary exams dismally.

I attended Honours Evening with a heavy heart. I didn't feel I belonged there. When the master of ceremonies announced that it was time for the matric awards, I could feel my heart beating two times faster than normal. As fate would have it, the first award given was a huge trophy for the Top English Student of the Year. It was presented by Ms D, one of the best teachers I have ever known in my life.

'This award goes to a diligent student, one of the best I have ever taught. She is an inquisitive young girl with an unusual love for books. It has been my great pleasure to teach such an inspiring organic intellectual. Ladies and gentlemen, please give a round of applause to Malaika Mahlatsi . . .'

I stood up to loud applause, terror gripping me. I kept expecting her to apologise for calling out the wrong name, waiting for that moment when I would be the laughing stock of the ceremony. It didn't happen. I walked onto the stage and hugged Ms D, one of the few teachers who had continued to believe in me even when I was barely passing anything. We hugged for what felt like hours, tears streaming down both our faces. She handed the huge trophy and certificate to me, as well as a gift bag she had purchased for me personally. The entire hall stood up to clap. I looked into the crowd with tears in my eyes and smiled.

The next trophy was also mine. By this time, I was no longer panicking. I was confident that I was getting what I deserved. I had performed dismally in my preliminary exams but that had been undermined by my year's average results, which factored in results from all terms. I'd not done too well in the first two terms but I had done well enough to make up for the dismal performance in the prelims. I'd managed to obtain a C+ average, which was boosted greatly by my A+ averages in English and Setswana. I was also awarded the EC Lindeque Trophy, awarded annually to 'the most promising senior student of the year'.

I knew I'd be alright. I would write my final exams and get into Stellenbosch University. I was going to be a nuclear scientist. I had not had a very easy life but maybe, just maybe, there was hope in the Rainbow Nation after all.

PART II

A kindled flame: Searching for a political home when the centre no longer holds

How Stellenbosch University changed me

I WROTE MY FINAL EXAMS without too much difficulty. I was able to catch up on some fundamental things and believed without doubt that I would pull through just fine. I had not applied to any other university but Stellenbosch because there was nowhere else I wanted to go. Many of my friends and my boyfriend were going to the University of the Witwatersrand. Daniel had decided to do Actuarial Science, Diana was going to study law and Kabelo was going to study medicine. Kgothatso, Palesa and Mpumi were all going to Vaal University of Technology to do Information Technology. I didn't want to be in Gauteng. I wanted to be in the Western Cape, at Stellenbosch University, doing a BSc in Physics.

In January 2010, our matric results came out. I hadn't got as many distinctions as I'd hoped for. I knew that English was a given, and I aced the subject with over 85 per cent, the highest result for English Home Language in the entire district. I missed distinctions in Setswana and History by 1 per cent. But I was proud of myself for having achieved a good average and an exemption with distinction.

A few days after receiving my matric results, I received a letter from Stellenbosch University informing me that while I had done relatively well in my admission tests, my Afrikaans mark was low. I was also a point short for admission to Nuclear Physics but I could always look at alternatives similar to that discipline. Taking into account the fact Nuclear Physics had negative implications for the continent anyway, I decided that I'd instead do Theoretical and Laser Physics. My mother had no money for bus fare, so she booked a train ticket for me. The twenty-six hour journey from Johannesburg to Cape Town was one of the best of my life. A friend of mine, Lungile, who was studying at Stellenbosch University, was going to wait for me at Cape Town Station. I read Dan Brown's *Digital Fortress* on the journey.

I arrived in the Western Cape feeling extremely tired. The plan was to stay with Lungile while I tried to sort out the change in my degree choices. I arrived in the Western Cape early to see the place before settling in. I intended to return home after a week to fetch the rest of the things I'd need.

Lungile was an incredible host but something happened to me while I was at the university. I felt out of place. I couldn't bring myself to like the campus. Noticing this change in me, Lungile did what she thought would solve the problem. Little did she know she'd only make it worse. She took me to a students' braai in the hopes I'd enjoy it and change my mind about the institution. But as I stood in the middle of what felt to me like a sea of blonde-haired, blue-eyed people speaking in Afrikaans, I knew that Stellenbosch University was not the place for me. I couldn't exist alongside conservative Afrikaaners who, by the look of things, still regarded us as kaffirs with whom they had no intention of even attempting to be polite.

Before my arrival in Stellenbosch, I hadn't been exposed to an environment dominated by Afrikaaners. I had interacted with some individuals here and there but never with them as a great collective in their own backyard. It was at this party that I first felt the magnitude of the contempt that Afrikaners have for us, a contempt that can be expressed in as minute a gesture as a glance.

The black students, few though they were at that braai, were huddled together in one corner, almost cowering from the marquee infested with their Afrikaaner counterparts. Four or five girls, whom Lindiwe introduced me to, sat at the far end of the festivities speaking, almost in a whisper, their mother tongue. It eluded me why they were isolating themselves so clearly until I walked towards the bar to get myself some lemonade.

The walk from that one end of the garden to the other felt like a march through the valley of the shadow of death.

Everywhere around me, pale skins were laughing, dancing and conversing in Afrikaans. I didn't hear a single word of another language. It was easy then to understand why the black students would feel marginalised to the point of sitting in a corner away from the crowd.

The young lady who was giving out drinks was called Marjorie—someone had called out her name at some point while I was standing in the queue—and she looked annoyed when she saw me. The look of mild irritation on her face was so stunning to me that for a few seconds I thought about getting out of the queue and returning to the girls. Something in me, a stubborness born from years of building confidence in myself, would not allow me to give her that satisfaction. So I stood in line and waited my turn.

When I finally reached the front of the queue, she asked me, almost angrily, 'Wat soek jy?'

Of course I knew what the question meant but I feigned puzzlement. I responded that I didn't understand the language she was speaking, and could immediately feel the unpleasant stares from other students around me boring down on me. She asked again, 'Wat soek jy?' and, again, I told her I didn't understand Afrikaans. Her response after that was angry almost to the point of an explosion. She asked, this time in English, 'What do you want?'

I said I wanted lemonade and she handed it to me. I walked away with a sense that her question had little to do with what I wanted to drink. I felt that what Marjorie was asking me was what I wanted in that place, on that campus, at that university. Something about the way she'd asked the question felt like an interrogation about not only what I wanted to drink but why I'd decided to dare to interrupt her world with my blackness.

I didn't tell Lungile about the incident, partly because I didn't want to make her feel guilty for having brought me to a party that had left me feeling depressed. Lungile was a sweet young woman who seemed to be comfortable with the status quo. She hadn't raised the issue of racism on the campus with me beyond making offhand remarks about how Afrikaans the university was. She appeared to have adapted to the conditions. I didn't think she'd understand how I felt.

I stayed in Stellenbosch University for a few more weeks, knowing deep in my heart that I would eventually have to leave because, try as I might, I couldn't picture my future at the institution. I called Daniel, who I was still seeing, and told him about my experience. We created a conference call to include Diana and Kabelo, our couple friends. I explained to all three of them that I wouldn't study at Stellenbosch but hadn't applied anywhere else and had nowhere to go if not Stellenbosch. Diana advised me to go back to Gauteng and try my luck at Wits University. I was sceptical. I had never liked Wits and I really didn't want to be there. I decided I'd rather try my luck with the University of the Western Cape but applications were closed and after trying to negotiate with the management, I was informed that the only space available was in Education. I didn't want to study towards a Bachelor of Education degree so I decided to return to Jo'burg and make up my mind once I got there what I was going to do with my life. I also knew how crushed my mother would be about my decision but I didn't allow that to change my mind. I wanted out.

One thing I knew the minute I walked out of the gates of Stellenbosch University was that my life would be dedicated to Black Consciousness activism. Stellenbosch confirmed to me a truth that I already knew about South Africa. It confirmed to me that not only is this country still trapped in the clutches of white racism but also that the struggle to free us from those clutches begged for the participation of all black people, particularly those of us who had had the privileged misfortune of being in multiracial institutions where we had had to deal with the ugly face of white supremacy on a daily basis. I could not wage that struggle alone within the institution but I hoped that by coming together with other like-minded young people, we would begin to at least ask critical questions and maybe, just maybe, we would be able to write a new narrative for and of blackness.

Searching for a political home in the abyss: The Blackwash and SNI experience

I HAD ALWAYS KNOWN that I would have a role to play in the development of black people but it was not until I walked out of the gates of Stellenbosch University that I knew exactly how I would make my mark in our struggle: I would join a radical Black Consciousness organisation and serve in its communications department. I was passionate about writing and communicating with people and I wanted to use my passion and talent to rewrite the black narrative.

On 16 June 2010, I attended a political event at Regina Mundi in Soweto, where I met a man who would play a critical role in my life. His name is Andile Mngxitama. I had been an avid reader of Andile's 'Bolekaja!' column in *The Sowetan*. I found Andile to be a very interesting and engaging individual. He had been friends with my mother at some point and it was she who had introduced me to his journal, *New Frank Talk*, which I had thoroughly enjoyed and found extremely radical. Andile was with a group of young people when I met him; they belonged to a radical Black Consciousness movement based in Soweto called Blackwash. Blackwash had been established by a group of radical Black Conscious feminists who had met at Rhodes University in Grahamstown years before. The initial idea was for the organisation to become a movement for black women but later that idea had been abandoned and Blackwash became a movement for young, angry and militant young people who wanted to revive and give a radical face to the comatose modern Black Consciousness Movement.

I knew immediately upon meeting the group that I wanted to join Blackwash. That first night, we sat discussing the writings of Bantu Steve Biko for hours. I had read his book, *I Write What I Like*, which my mother had bought for me as a present for my birthday. The awkwardness that often occurs when one first meets a group of strangers was non-existent. From the point of introductions, we got along like long-lost friends. My horrendous experience at Stellenbosch University had transformed me into a very angry individual.

I was angry at myself for having applied to study at the institution. I was angry at the institution for having accepted my application. I was angry at my mother for not warning me about the potential danger that lay ahead of me in the Western Cape, the danger of facing an untransformed community of conservative right-wing Afrikaners. Above all, I was angry at the Rainbow Nation once again. I had fallen for the romantic rhetoric as a child, believing that Model-C schools were a haven for everyone. And there I was again, falling for the same lie that institutions of higher learning are accommodating of everyone, irrespective of class, background or ideological orientation. I was angry at you, the ANC-led government, for painting a false picture of South Africa. A South Africa of genuine social cohesion and racial harmony did not exist. It does not exist. Blackwash, with its anti-white politics, was exactly the kind of movement an eighteen-year-old angry black girl from the township could identify with, because there are times when the only weapon a black child can use to fight against a system that dehumanises her is to be so angry that she is left with no choice but to dare to be alive. Anger, for many of us, has been a driver of our ideas, at times even more so than the love for our people.

Within a few weeks of joining the organisation, I was already in the inner circle. Andile was the ultimate leader of the movement, followed by two of its founders, Zandi 'Zeer' Radebe and Ncebakazi 'Ncesh' Manzi, who had both graduated from Rhodes University, with master's and honours degrees respectively. Zandi and Ncesh were extremely intelligent young women with a strong passion for the black struggle. They took me under their wings, feeding me the literature that had inspired their thinking and politics. I was introduced to the writings of Assata Shakur, a radical African-American woman who is exiled in Cuba. Assata is one of the leading figures of the Black Panther movement, which emerged in the later stages of the Civil Rights Movement in the United States. It advocated the use of weapons and violence. On a number of occasions these threats were made good. The militant and radical factions demonstrated to the masses that a small segment of the Civil Rights Movement had the capacity to apply brute force where necessary. Assata was arrested by the American government on a false charge of murder and, subsequently, escaped prison to find refuge from Fidel Castro's anti-imperialist government. Currently on the Federal Bureau of Investigation's Most Wanted list and with a price on her head, Assata still resides in Cuba, where the socialist government is protecting her from the claws of US intelligence.

I was also introduced to the writings of Frantz Fanon, Sékou Touré, Frank B. Wilderson, Dr Chinweizu and many other critical and radical writers with a particular focus on defining 'the nervous conditions of blackness'—Fanon described the colonial position as being a sickness.

I was soon made an administrator of the movement, tasked with ensuring the smooth running of day-to-day duties, such as responding to emails and writing press statements. When it was discovered that I was gifted in the art of writing, Andile asked me to assist Ncesh with the research for and editing of *New Frank Talk*. I was over the moon. *New Frank Talk* was a popular journal doing very well in terms of sales. It was a great honour for me to be entrusted with assisting its editor with research and writing.

Shortly after beginning to assist Ncesh with *New Frank Talk*, I was asked by Andile to participate in a project called the September National Imbizo. The SNI had been birthed on Facebook when people who shared the same views as Blackwash proposed a national conference where radical black minds would converge to plot a path for the black struggle. I agreed. A week later, a task team for SNI was appointed and a meeting was held at Moletsane High School in Soweto. The task team was divided into four departments: content and ideological work; finance and fundraising; logistics and marketing; and public relations. Andile advised me to join the content and ideological work team, which was comprised of three other people, namely himself, Ncesh and a very bold man named Jackie Shandu. The four of us were responsible for political work and, to some degree, governance. Our immediate mandate was to draft discussion documents for the SNI, which we had decided would take place that September, less than three months away. How we imagined we would pull it off defies logic.

Preparations for the SNI began immediately after the meeting in Moletsane. The content and ideological work team met regularly at Andile's office in Braamfontein to discuss and brainstorm the discussion documents. It was during this period of drafting documents that I was appointed as the secretary general of the SNI. I became the signatory on the SNI bank accounts and sat in the driving seat of power within the organisation. I knew that there were people who were displeased about my quick rise to power within the movement but at the time I believe I'd earned the position. I was the youngest member of the core and one of the most committed. By then I was enrolled at the University of South Africa, a long-distance learning institution. I had a lot of time on my hands as I didn't have to attend any lectures. All that time was dedicated to the work of the SNI and Blackwash. The movement had become my life.

Shortly before the end of the 2010 FIFA Soccer World Cup tournament hosted in South Africa, Blackwash decided to run an anti-Afrophobia campaign across the country. This campaign was informed by reports and speculation that the so-called xenophobic violence of 2008 would recur just after the tournament. Being a Black Consciousness and pan-Africanist movement, we decided that we would not allow a situation where our African brothers and sisters would find themselves at the mercy of angry South African mobs without doing our best to avert the potential catastrophe. After a few days of brainstorming, we had a coherent plan of action and a solid programme. We decided to run political education campaigns on the streets to educate ordinary citizens of our country about why African nationals shouldn't be attacked.

We prepared pamphlets from Andile's office and various Internet cafes around the central business district. Blackwash didn't have an office, so we relied on our own equipment, such as laptops and cellphones. For access to the Internet, we relied on Internet cafes and Andile's office. The campaign was called Singamakwerekwere Sonke!, meaning 'We are all foreigners'. 'Amakwerekwere' is a derogatory term that is often used in townships to refer to non-South Africans. The tragedy about this labelling is that it is used selectively. Whites who are not natives of our country are never referred to as 'Amakwerekwere'; it is only blacks who are given this dehumanising label. By calling the campaign Singamakwerekwere Sonke! we wanted to expose just how ridiculous it is to call our own people that, since all Africans are one.

Singamakwerekwere Sonke! was marketed and popularised on social media. The page created specifically for the campaign had almost three thousand followers and the majority of them identified with the politics of Blackwash. The campaign seemed to have the support of many people and we were convinced that on the day of national action we'd have masses on the streets. If I knew then what I know now about social media and its ability to deceive, I would have insisted that we work harder at mobilising established community-based organisations and NGOs with similar politics to our own. But at that time I was naïve, believing that the social media numbers would translate to numbers on the ground. It was not to be. On the day scheduled for mass action across the country, with campaigns happening across major cities in all provinces, a group of us converged at the Mary Fitzgerald Square in Newtown, Johannesburg. We had expected at least a hundred people to join us in Gauteng but fewer than fifteen people arrived, and most of whom had been in the organising committee of the campaign. It was a disappointing turnout. Andile made the suggestion that we call off the protest but we were able to convince him that it was not the numbers that counted but the message we were sending out. Eventually he agreed that we'd find a way to deploy people to critical areas to hand out pamphlets and engage the people on the issues we were raising. Three groups of four were assembled. One would go to Bree taxi rank, another to Noord taxi rank and another to Hillbrow. We had wanted to go to Diepsloot, the epicentre of the 2008 xenophobic violence, but we did not have the necessary numbers and we knew just how dangerous it would be to attempt to go there when we were so few.

Three of my colleagues and I were deployed to Noord taxi rank, which is now known as MTN Rank, in the Jo'burg CBD. It was me, Andile Mngxitama, Marechera Wa Ndata and a young woman named Katlego, who had travelled from the Vaal. We began to distribute the pamphlets to commuters and taxi drivers, with Andile and me speaking to people one by one, telling them why it was wrong to attack and kill our African brothers and sisters. Most of the people listened but some were very hostile and told us to go to hell. One taxi driver confronted me and in a very angry voice said, 'The reason you want us to not kill these people is because you are being fucked by Nigerians . . .'

At this, Andile and Marechera ran to my defence. Not long after that, the three of us were grabbed by the collars of our shirts by three armed men. We were dragged up the stairs to a room near the taxi rank. Our pamphlets were confiscated. We were subjected to an interrogation for what felt like decades. The three men swore at us, intimidated us and threatened to assault us. They accused us of wanting to turn the country into a haven for 'foreigners', who they accused of being responsible for escalating crime levels and unemployment. Eventually they let us go but kept our pamphlets. I was eighteen years old at the time, terrified beyond measure, hungry, cold and feeling disappointed by the refusal of our people to understand the importance of our cause.

We met up with the rest of the group at Nikki's Oasis, a

small restaurant and bar just across from the Market Theatre. That night, we sat and discussed the state of our continent. We all felt extremely dejected. That was one of the first of many moments in my life where I learned that it is going to be a very long walk to mental freedom for our people. The sheer magnitude of resentment expressed towards our own people reflected more than the conditions of inequalities that were at the heart of the Afrophobia that was steadily increasing in the country. It was a vivid picture of a people deeply colonised. My idealism, my belief in the inherent goodness of black people was tested greatly on that day and as we sat conducting a postmortem on our failed campaign, I could see clearly the hard work that awaited us, work that we might not manage to get through in our lifetime.

By the time we left Nikki's, we were in a state of defeatism, engulfed by sadness.

—◦—

A few days later, everyone had sobered up. We knew that we had to work ten times harder to ensure the success of the SNI, which by then was two months away. The discussion documents were not complete, registration of delegates was slow and there was not a single cent in our coffers. Ncesh and I agreed that I would move into her apartment in town and together we would work on the completion of the documents and other important aspects of the Imbizo. I had no computer of my own and the laptop I had been lent by one of our group members wasn't working properly. My mother was very supportive of my political activities so when I informed her that I'd be staying with Ncesh for a few weeks, she gave me her blessings. Ncesh was staying with her younger sister Funeka, a member of Blackwash who didn't possess the same passion or dedication to the cause as her sister. Despite this, Funeka was a very pleasant individual and we got along very well. The three of us shared the bachelor apartment together. Andile would bring us food every night because we hardly had time or money to spare. We woke up early and went to sleep late. We had five books to read between us, complex political literature that demanded a lot of time and attention to detail.

A month before the SNI was to take place, disaster struck. I had a public disagreement with one of the executive members of the team, Kagiso Monnapula. Kagiso had posted on Facebook that 'foreign' nationals were the cause of rising levels of poverty and unemployment in the townships because they did not fight against exploitation and so employers preferred them over South African nationals, who were famous for protesting for salary increases. I was livid! Just a few days before that, we had run a campaign fighting against this kind of thinking and now one of our own was expressing an opinion we'd completely rejected and had diagnosed as a problem. I commented on the post, accusing Kagiso of being a hypocrite, to which he retaliated by accusing me of being holier-than-thou and afflicted with an exaggerated sense of self-importance. This led to a serious confrontation between the two of us, witnessed by thousands of people who were now following Blackwash and SNI activities very closely.

By the time Andile called both of us to order, the damage had been done. SNI was divided, with some people taking my side and some siding with Kagiso. Until that moment, I had had no idea at all that anyone in the organisation had a problem with me. But it came out that people had been harbouring resentment towards me because I was seen to be arrogant and self-righteous. After the fight with Kagiso, I had a disagreement with Zandi, one of the leaders of the movement. She had been bullying everyone for a long time and being the stubborn individual that life had made of me, I refused to be one of her statistics. Andile was conflicted; he didn't know how to handle the situation because he was very close to both of us. His delay in acting resulted in two prominent factions emerging. The faction led by Zandi was dominated by members of the organisation from Soweto and the opposing faction was dominated by the rest of the members, who were in the majority. The Soweto faction, despite its small numbers, was extremely radical where the other faction was comprised mainly of intellectuals and theoreticians. The movement was at war with itself and it was ugly.

I had never been in a political organisation before and had no clue how to deal with politics of factions and cabals. If I had known then what I know now, I would've realised that, in many ways, I was responsible for the legitimisation of this factionalism. Because I was angry at Zandi and what I believed to be her faction, I withdrew from them and only associated myself with those who were in the opposite camp, mainly Ncesh. This act of immaturity, when I look at it in retrospect, could have been prevented had the sizes of our egos been reduced from the size of Antarctica to the size of Swaziland.

It was during this dark period in the organisation that I was approached by a prominent NGO in Johannesburg called Khanya College. Established in the mid-1980s, Khanya had evolved from being an educational institution for political activists to focusing on social justice politics and the training of other NGOs and trade unions. Khanya needed people who would assist with the Jozi Book Fair, an annual event for small publishers, writers and poets. I liked the work that Khanya was doing and had immense respect for its director, a Marxist–Leninist activist named Oupa Lehulere. I agreed to work at Khanya College. It was while working there that one of my mother's former colleagues, Mark Weinberg, asked me to consider doing an internship at yet another Marxist–Leninist organisation based in Cape Town. The offer sounded good. I would be tasked with writing and editing, two fields I was growing passionate about. The Alternative Information and Development Centre (AIDC) had seen my work published by Khanya College and was interested in employing me as an intern.

I was very excited despite knowing very little about Marxism–Leninism, an ideology that was greatly rejected by Blackwash, on the basis that it was foreign. But I was also sceptical about taking up the offer because I had had a public spat with one of the board members of the organisation, Mazibuko Jara. Mazibuko and I had fought over Andile. Or, rather, I had taken Andile's side in one of their disagreements and, wanting to impress him with my loyalty, had humiliated Mazibuko before the eyes of the social media audience. I viewed Mazibuko Jara, a man I'd never met, through the same lenses through which Andile viewed him, and an enemy of Andile was an enemy of the revolution and, therefore, of myself, so deep was my loyalty to the man.

It took me a few days to muster the courage but, ultimately, I informed Andile and other members of the committee that I was contemplating joining the AIDC. As expected, the news was not well received. I could sense Andile's fury and disappointment in me for contemplating joining what he called 'liberal Marxists and white supremacists'. But I had reached a point where I had decided that I refused to feel like Andile's stooge anymore. A sense of purpose had found its way into my conscience and I was determined to define myself outside of Blackwash. I had realised the need for the movement to grow beyond the cult of one man and decided that I would no longer fight Andile's battles and I would not continue alienating everyone who didn't see eye to eye with our movement. If the movement was to grow, we needed to form strategic alliances with the progressive left. I said this much to Andile. I had no way of knowing that this decision would sink me politically in Blackwash and the SNI.

A few weeks before the SNI was scheduled to take place, I was removed as the secretary general. To this day, I don't know precisely why I was removed and I doubt that a serious reason could be provided by those who made the decision to remove me.

I was sitting at home with my mother one Sunday afternoon when I received a call from Ncesh telling me that there was a committee meeting taking place that day. I was surprised about this because, as the secretary general, coordinating meetings was my responsibility. And yet there I was, receiving calls from other committee members telling me about meetings I had no idea about. At that point in time, I was not too worried. I knew that there was a lot of tension in the organisation, which would explain the strange behaviour of usually reasonable comrades like Ncesh. Floating in my own naivety, I didn't think that anyone would sabotage me. I was producing work that very few people could pull off. But more than that, the SNI was only a few weeks away and I was a signatory on all the financial accounts. It would be disastrous for me to be removed as the secretary general because that would mean that the signatories would have to be changed, a process that would demand more time than we had on our hands. It was too much administration and no one had the time or energy to pursue such an unnecessary task. Or so I thought.

Before I could decide whether or not to gatecrash the meeting, I was paid a visit by Ncesh and Zuki, the head of the fundraising committee, who came to formally inform me that I couldn't sit in on the meeting or any other from that point forward. I asked what the reason for this was and Ncesh told me that other members of the committee felt 'uncomfortable' in my presence.

'Why would anyone feel uncomfortable in my presence? I have been working with these people very closely for the last few months. How do they wake up today feeling uncomfortable in my presence?' I asked Ncesh.

She didn't give me a convincing answer and at that point I didn't probe any further. I realised, with a sinking heart, that the unthinkable had happened: Andile, fearing that I was becoming uncontrollable, had lobbied members of the committee to agree unanimously to my removal. I had seen him doing this to other people. I had *helped* him do this to others before. We had dealt many brilliant radical people the same blow. Their names started ringing in my head. Their only crime had been that they had openly and publicly disagreed with Andile, the same way I had been doing over the past few weeks.

I was removed as the secretary general of the SNI less than two weeks before the National Imbizo. I did not fight this decision. I knew I had two options: to go back and beg Andile for forgiveness for being true to my own principles or to leave Blackwash and find another political home. I did not want to join your Youth League or any other component of the Mass Democratic Movement and I knew very little about other organisations. But I had to leave Blackwash because staying meant I would have to concede to what I felt was being Andile's puppet, as were all those who were in the organisation. I would not subject myself to that life. The thought of it was too excruciating.

The September National Imbizo took place in Soweto. It was a three-day event. I only attended on the Saturday. I didn't want to go on Friday, the day of registration, because I didn't think I would be accredited. The thought of being humiliated in the presence of other people didn't go down well with me, and so I resolved that I would gatecrash the Imbizo the following day, where only accredited delegates were expected to show up. I believed I ran a greater risk of being hauled off the property on registration day than I did on the day where commissions would be taking place. Plus, I reasoned to myself, if I was to be kicked out on the day of registration, I wouldn't know how the discussions about the important issues contained in the document that Ncesh and I had spent long hours working on went.

What I witnessed there convinced me that there was no hope for the movement. I felt that there was very little substance to the politics engaged. For the first time since I'd joined Blackwash a few months before, I realised just how anarchic our members were. Misdirected venom was being spewed everywhere. In commissions, discussions were degenerating into contests of vulgarities. Everyone seemed to have made a calamitous retreat from thinking and reasoning intelligently. Some delegates were drunk and some had not even read the discussion documents, judging by the lack of content in the arguments that were being posed. When one participant suggested that one of the resolutions of the Imbizo ought to be a radical demand of R8 billion from Coca-Cola—to wild applause—I knew that the SNI was not serious. Everyone was throwing around rhetoric and not coming up with a coherent and sustainable plan of action on how to address the nervous black condition that is sinking our people deeper into poverty and destitution. The SNI had failed to generate or direct intelligent discourse.

I was angry. I was devastated beyond measure, not only because the SNI that had presented hope for young township people like myself had disintegrated before it could attempt to define itself, but because such disintegration only served to re-awaken the nagging fear I had, that perhaps the key to the emancipation of the black nation lay in swelling your ranks and contesting the terrain of progressive discourse. But just the idea that there existed a possibility that it was you, the ANC, that could rewrite the black narrative sounded extremely vulgar to me. The SNI had been stillborn but surely that didn't mean that there was no vehicle, somewhere out there, moving in the direction of the left. Surely.

At the end of September, I packed my bags and left for

Cape Town. I had accepted the offer to complete an internship programme at the AIDC. The organisation was going to pay for my accommodation in Cape Town, my flight and everything else I would need. I was also going to earn a very generous monthly stipend, which, because I had no responsibilities outside providing for myself, was rather quite a lot. But, more than this, I would be doing work that I enjoyed. It was the beginning of a new chapter in the story of my life as a young person seeking to be rooted in civil society politics.

———•◦•———

For the most part I was happy at the AIDC though it was not at all what I had imagined it would be. I had expected to be in a radical space with energetic minds bloated with the same idealism as me. Instead, I found myself in an environment that bordered on the conservative. I was immediately drawn to three of the staff members, a young intern named Mzulungile Cabanga, a senior project coordinator named Thembeka Majali, who was an activist belonging to the pan-Africanist bloc, and the receptionist, Noma, who was like a mother to all of us. The four of us were like a family. Every morning we had tea together and almost every weekend I was either with Mzu or with sis Thembeka, who had taken me under her wing to teach me the politics of the civic sector.

I was uneasy about the politics of the AIDC because beneath their progressiveness I detected the malignant cancer of racism. Brian Ashley, the director, was a progressive activist who had sharpened his teeth in the Black Consciousness Movement in the 1980s and Mark Weinberg, his deputy, was a humanist with a passion for peace and unity. But I always felt—and maybe I am too harsh on the gentlemen—that Brian in particular had not fully shed his whiteness.

This unease was reinforced when, later in my internship, we started organising public forums as part of our Media Advocacy Programme. The forums were a spectacle of white arrogance, where blacks appeared to serve as nothing more than a spectator audience tasked with rubber-stamping decisions and positions of the so-called progressive left, dominated by white intellectual activists. We were always inviting community-based organisations to our forums, where speaker after speaker pitched debate at a level that was clearly above our mainly grassroots black activists. One forum in particular made me snap. It was a discussion on the National Health Insurance that the government was proposing, and we wanted to have a forum reflective of the civil society movement.

The panelists of the discussion were, again, mainly white intellectuals. They went on and on about what the consequences of that system of healthcare would be. The discussion was highly technical and you'd expect the people engaging in so complex a subject to have at least read the discussion document but this was not the case. What we had instead were young people, some not even out of high school. The adults there were clearly not familiar with the document that was being discussed either. It seemed obvious to me from their failure to ask important questions that this was a rent-a-crowd group of grassroots activists, tasked with the responsibility of agreeing to everything that was being suggested by the funder of their trip—the AIDC. I was livid!

After the forum ended, I confronted my colleagues, asking them why they'd treated the poor with such arrogant contempt by reducing them to mere decorations in a forum whose outcome had been long determined by those white intellectuals. When no one was able to respond, I went to Brian and asked him the same question.

'Had these people even seen this document before this evening, Brian? Did we send it to them by email a week prior to the forum?'

Brian admitted that we hadn't. I asked, 'What, then, was the point of having them here, when they were not even afforded an opportunity to examine what they were being bussed in to discuss? Are we so contemptuous of the poor, so arrogant in our thinking, that we don't believe we owe it to them to engage them on an equal footing?'

Because we had some cleaning up to do, Brian requested I come into his office the following day to discuss the issue in more detail. I was so angry I almost responded by showing my middle finger. Sense prevented this but when I turned away from him I was no longer able to view the AIDC the same way.

The meeting the following day did nothing to alleviate my anger. I'd come face to face with the ugly truth that Blackwash and SNI had long diagnosed: that white supremacy is so deeply entrenched that even the most progressive of white people still suffer from it. I had concluded the previous night that there was an urgent need for me to return to dedicating my energies to the Black Consciousness bloc. It was vital for my sanity.

I completed my internship at the AIDC in December 2010

but stayed one more month in Cape Town deciding where I wanted to propel my politics. I wanted to be sure this time that when I dived into a movement that appeared to be championing the cause that I was so passionate about, I would not regret the decision. I wasn't content with the white progressives that I'd been exposed to and had no intention of a repeated experience with misguided black militants.

When I returned to Johannesburg in January 2011, I threw myself into community work at Khanya College, taking up employment as a field worker in the Jozi Book Fair department. I will cherish that experience for the rest of my life because it was there that I learned the importance of allowing communities to be involved in creating their own solutions to their own struggles. Khanya College could never be accused of treating the poor like decorations. In Oupa Lehulere, I found a mentor, a comrade and a role model.

Julius Malema's influence on my political worldview

EVEN AFTER THE DEJECTING EXPERIENCE that I went through with Blackwash and the September National Imbizo, I still wanted to believe that the pan-Africanist and Black Consciousness bloc was my political home. I wondered many a time if I was not misplaced in a bloc that seemed more obsessed with the perpetuation of apartheid nostalgia than with giving birth to new ideas that would provide solutions to the ongoing violence of black existence.

There were times when I sat on my own contemplating my political direction. During those times, thoughts of joining your party engulfed my mind. I would often take an A4 sheet of paper and divide it into two equal halves. On the one side I would write 'Reasons to join the ANC' and on the other 'Reasons not to join the ANC'. The second side of the paper always had more points than the first, confirming to me that my politics were more reflective of the Black Consciousness and pan-Africanist school of thought than they were of the narrow nationalist ideological posture that I believed you reflected. I would thus talk myself out of the temptation of being part of the Congress Movement, encouraged by the words of Dr Kwame Nkrumah, the former prime minister and, later, president of Ghana, who said, 'The total liberation and unification of Africa under an All-African Socialist Government must be the primary objective of all black revolutionaries throughout the world. It is an objective which, when achieved, will bring about the fulfilment of the aspirations of Africans and people of African descent everywhere. It will at the same time advance the triumph of the international socialist movement.'

I didn't think that you espoused this, or that your orientation was the same. And yet somehow a part of me continued to harbour sentiments of my childhood growing up in a community loyal to the Congress Movement.

I decided that before I joined any organisation, I would conduct thorough research about it and only when I understood its policies and had gone through its discussion documents, I would join it. I was under the impression that by the end of this quest, I would have been swayed towards either the Pan Africanist Congress of Azania, the Socialist Party of Azania or the Azanian People's Organisation. If anyone had told me at this point that the organisation whose policies I would identify with was in the Congress Movement, I would have laughed at them.

It was while I was contemplating the direction that my political life would take that I found my attention captured by the then president of the African National Congress Youth League, comrade Julius Malema. I had been following his work with great fascination. He represented everything I believed the youth of this country should represent: a die-hard spirit and fearlessness that knew no limits. But it was when, under his leadership, the ANCYL championed the call for the nationalisation of mines that I began to have immense respect for comrade Malema. For the first time in a very long time, I found myself identifying with the politics of the ANCYL.

Not since the unprecedented recalling of former African National Congress and state president Mr Thabo Mbeki, had the country's collective attention been as captured as it was by the ANC Youth League's radical call for the nationalisation of mines. Those opposed to this call argued that nationalisation would serve the interests of capital by bailing out indebted capitalists who are losing profits as a result of the 2008 global financial recession. Those in support of this call saw it as a vehicle that will drive the country towards addressing the triple challenges of unemployment, poverty and unequal spatial development. There is also a portion of the population that supported the concept of nationalisation, albeit not as defined and proposed by the ANCYL. These people argued that if the method proposed by the ANCYL was employed,

South Africa would 'become another Zimbabwe'. This argument didn't convince me, because I knew of countries, like Zambia, where it was the privatisation of mines, not their nationalisation, that had led to poverty and unemployment.

I belong to the bloc that supported the call for the nationalisation of mines and the expropriation of land without compensation. It had always irked me that we live in a country where a settler minority is holding an entire native population to ransom, keeping it in chains of economic bondage. Billions of rands were being made in our extractive economy. Minerals and other raw materials were profiting a few while many suffered the cruelty of poverty.

The land question is also one close to my heart. I find it atrocious that less than 10 per cent of the population controlled more than two-thirds of the land in a country where natives are subjected to RDP houses and concentration camps in the form of informal settlements. And to suggest that the government had to buy back this land is absurd to me. Nothing about our history made it correct that a black-led government should be exhausting resources on the purchasing of land that rightfully belonged to the people.

But I understood the complex dynamics behind the call by the ANC Youth League. I understood that because of centuries of being systematically ostracised from the political economy of land, black people are not prepared for radical land and agrarian reform. The reality of the situation is that owning land is not as romantic as land rights activists make it sound. It is not just about black families having hectares of land to themselves. It is also about the ability to sustain that land, to ensure productivity and maximise utilisation. It is also about ensuring that there is a market for whatever is being produced. Farming is not easy, or cheap. It demands a lot of resources and skills and expertise, which, unfortunately, most black people don't have as a result of their not having grown up in an environment that nurtured a love for farming.

There are many white kids who grow up on farms or whose parents have farms they use as vacation homes. Their love for farming is a product of this socialisation. If you were to give someone like me, a person who grew up in Soweto and who knows nothing about farm life, a farm today, what exactly could I do with it? I've never spent any time on a farm and know almost nothing about farming.

We don't have vegetable gardens in our townships; few homes even have flower gardens. Our yards are concrete and the closest thing to farming that we do is water the small grass patches we call gardens.

So I understood that the call for land expropriation, correct though it was, was more sentimental than pragmatic. But I supported it and I was willing to defend it, because it was a necessary discussion for our nation to enter into.

Despite my warming up to the radical shift in the politics of the Youth League, I was still very sceptical about joining it. But I admired the leadership of comrade Malema and knew that if there was ever a time for me to join your Congress Movement, this was it. The youth movement wouldn't be as dynamic in a very long time as it was under comrade Malema. It had taken decades for the Youth League to arrive at a point of such militancy. This was a defining moment in the politics of our country, at least in so far as the role of the youth was concerned. The youth was agitating for something powerful beyond measure, and even if there was an element of naivety in the cause that was being fought, there was also an element of revolutionarism that demanded to be understood.

A few months after his unopposed re-election, the parameters of the demise of comrade Julius Malema were plotted, by himself and by you. Newspapers were bombarding us with stories about his possible suspension from the ANC Youth League following some 'reckless' statements that he had made about the sitting government of Botswana being a 'puppet regime' and a 'footstool of imperialism' on the African continent. Comrade Julius had dared to make the bold assertion that the Youth League would send a command team to assist opposition parties to remove the ruling party from office. From a diplomatic point of view, this was a big faux pas. The Youth League had no mandate to make such pronouncements, as its task is to mobilise the youth under your banner and to agitate for policy shift from within. But the truth will out, and that truth is that many of us felt this way about the Botswana government. A year later, I would journey into working with civil society youth movements trying to put pressure on the stubborn Botswana government to ratify and domesticate the African Youth Charter, and would find myself reflecting back on comrade Julius's correct arguments.

On 1 March 2012, South Africa woke up to headlines announcing comrade Julius's expulsion. The news sent shockwaves throughout the country. Many of us who had been following the developments of the case since August of the previous year had expected him to be suspended, not expelled. He had the option of appealing the sentence with your National Disciplinary Committee of Appeals, or of employing delay tactics that would drag the matter on until the Mangaung elective congress in December of that year, from where he could mobilise delegates with voting powers to have the sanction nullified. But it didn't look likely that the sentence would be changed, and so many of us reconciled ourselves to the reality that the ANC Youth League was losing one of its greatest potential leaders.

The downfall of comrade Malema hit me harder than I could have imagined, perhaps because there was something in him that had represented something that I identified with. There were many things about comrade Julius that I didn't agree with. I found him to be an insufferable male chauvinist, an opinion I had formed during Jacob Zuma's rape trial. Having led the 'Friends of Jacob Zuma' brigade, Malema had been at the forefront of the onslaught against the woman who had laid the charges against Mr Zuma, accusing her of being a pawn in a political game and lying about the alleged sexual assault. I also didn't agree with how he addressed his elders. A level of respect must be maintained at all times when engaging elders, no matter how much one's opinion differs from theirs. This is a principle I believe in and one that comrade Malema clearly does not. And yet, despite all this, I believed strongly that comrade Julius was a rough diamond that needed polishing. In him, I saw the future of South Africa, and that future was a triumphant one.

One evening, as I sat on my bed, I found myself in tears

over what was happening to him. In many ways, I was crying for the many voiceless poor black people who now no longer had someone to speak on their behalf, someone who understood the brutality of the black condition. You had long forgotten what that condition looked like. It ended when you institutionalised maladministration and corruption, two cancers that eat away at the moral fibre of our society. It ended when you decided that it was correct to recall a sitting president who had done a lot for the development of our country. Some argued that comrade Julius too was a vessel that carried this cancer, that he too was corrupt. I didn't want to get into debates that couldn't be rooted in evidence. Sure, he tended to be vulgar in his opulence, buying and demolishing properties in affluent neighbourhoods, driving around in luxurious cars, drinking expensive liquor in the exorbitant restaurants and bars that he frequented. And in many ways, this was wrong. But comrade Malema was the closest thing to ourselves than anyone else at that point. He understood and articulated our struggles in ways that no one else could, because he knew them. He had lived those conditions. He identified with millions of us in townships who wanted nothing more than to not have to worry about where the next meal would come from.

In a state of anger, I took to Facebook. What I said at the time was that I wanted to challenge young people to view the ANC situation outside the cemented axis of interpretation that had been created by the media as well as the leadership and membership of both the ANC and the ANCYL: that Malema was reaping what he was responsible for sowing. This axis argued that, for a while, Malema had been wreaking havoc within the Alliance, taking part in 'reckless' behaviour that sought to undermine the ANC leadership and obliterate the culture of revolutionary discipline cemented in the oldest liberation movement on the African continent. The opposite side argued differently: that Malema was the fall guy in a savage game of dog-eat-dog politicking. That side alleged that Malema was paying the price for raising legitimate questions of those who benefit from having these questions out of public discourse, namely, you, the leadership of the ANC.

For those of us not privy to the internal matters of the ANC and its Youth League and who equally reject the often sensationalist interpretations of the media, the responsibility of dissecting the ANC crisis was left to our individual consciousness. I sought to look at the situation not from the angle of politicking but rather from a sociological perspective, viewing Malema as a person located within our society but with a political home within that society.

Malema could have been saved by many people at many points in his political journey but the chances were deliberately missed. The result of this was that a person who had immense potential to help Azania rewrite its narrative was dealt a political blow, making it virtually impossible for the audience who *needed* to listen to what he had to say to do so.

Malema was accused by the ANC NDC, the ANC leadership, membership and the general population of being the cause of the state of decay in the ANC. He was accused of being the cancer that infected and paralysed the Mass Democratic Movement. Some people even went as far as to claim that the decrease in the number of votes that the ANC had received at the previous elections was a direct result of Malema's radical pronouncements over the past few years. I believed these assertions were an attempt to use Malema as a scapegoat for a problem that is of our collective creation and one that could and should have been addressed at its infancy.

In 2008, a year when the country was thrown into a dark abyss, Julius Malema emerged as a hero of a faction that was hell-bent on utilising any means necessary to remove what it saw as a problem in the ANC. At one particular event attended by ANC and Youth League leaders and members, Julius Malema had this to say: 'The problem in this country is Thabo Mbeki and his people'. By this, Malema meant that the then president of the Republic of South Africa, Mr Mbeki, and his administration were the cause of the problems that the country was facing, socioeconomic and otherwise. Malema led a vicious campaign to unseat a constitutionally elected president, using methods unbecoming in a comrade, methods that ought to have left a bitter taste in the mouths of authentic patriots. Interestingly, at this point, at the zenith of his bad behaviour, Malema was not seen to be ill-disciplined or reckless. He was defined as a militant young person who spoke truth to power. We all clapped hands when he spoke, even when he was insulting elders. Archbishop Desmond Tutu once said, 'When you are neutral in situations of injustice, you have chosen the side of the oppressor'. This statement is most apt in capturing the response of our society to Malema's behaviour. We either justified his actions as being those of 'a radical young person' or we simply dismissed him with a shrug, never analysing the implications of our apathetic reaction to his uncouth behaviour.

Malema at the time seemed to be in the shadow of his political death. He faced an expulsion from an organisation he had dedicated years of his life to, an organisation that he poignantly called his 'home'. Many people were sitting comfortably in their corners with smirks on their faces, saying, 'He is ill-disciplined and must go!' Few used the opportunity to reflect upon *their* role in Malema's demise, which they didn't realise had implications beyond the settling of political vendettas.

It cannot be debated that under Malema, the ANCYL reintroduced the one issue that this country has consistently ostracised from political discourse: the race question. The ANCYL under Malema came out with guns blazing, guns pointed at the enemy: the system that survives on the subjugation of black people, the system that has institutionalised Afrophobia. The rapture that was created by the ANCYL under Malema was necessary, because it forced all of us to examine our location within an Azania that cunningly buries truths in favour of reconciliatory approaches to solving urgent matters. That rapture was the reason for the slow build-up of confidence that became evident in a people who had almost forgotten that they had a place in this anti-black world.

Indeed, Malema was not innocent in all this. But, I believed, *none* of us was. We must, as a people, realise that it is our responsibility to put an end to the convenient politicking that is rapidly manifesting on the African continent. I could see that as a people, whether as activists or as the general population, we need to begin to condemn ill-discipline in its elementary stages, whether or not it benefits our objectives, because ill-discipline *for* us soon becomes ill-discipline *against* us. The result of our failure to address it in its infancy is that at some point it is going to threaten revolutionary gains.

I realised that student organisations, as factories where future leaders are manufactured, should lead the revolution of the annihilation of ill-discipline. It begins with fighting against SRC corruption and misappropriation of resources. It begins with ceasing the culture of electing leaders on the basis of popularity as opposed to electing them on the basis of capacity to deliver. But, more than that, it begins with all of us standing united in the struggle, which is a quest for the cleansing of a society that we want our own children to grow up in. We cannot continue to let problems manifest and only at the height of their development react to them. In Sesotho we say, thupa e kojoa e sale metsi.

My anger withered away as the months went by. I had come to accept that our country was not ready for the rapture that it was going to experience someday. I knew from this moment that there would come a time, in my lifetime, when youth militancy would be inevitable. It was clear to me that the downfall of comrade Julius had postponed this country's fate. But fate cannot be fought. Someday, the South African youth was going to rise against you, because there was nothing normal about the situation in the ANC-led country. Nothing.

Finding a space for Africanism in a liberal university

BY THIS TIME I WAS A REGISTERED first-year student at Rhodes University. I had been able to access a higher education that, under this current system, hundreds of thousands of young black people never will. The militant Youth League of Malema had planted in me a seed that was refusing to be left unwatered. I had grown obsessed with the land and agrarian question and knew that if there was any real contribution I could make to the ongoing struggle of blackness against this oppressive system, it would have to be in rewriting the narrative of native identity. I had since determined that the rewriting of this narrative depends on giving back our people their source of dignity: the land. If I was going to be an activist, I would be a land and agrarian rights activist both on the ground and academically. I registered for a Bachelor of Social Science degree majoring in Earth Sciences/Geography and Economics, and took up two electives, Sociology and Anthropology.

I arrived in Grahamstown with great determination to participate in student politics. By this time I had been introduced to the politics of the Congress Movement at student level. The year before I went to the university, I had been an invited guest at the 24th National Congress of the ANCYL at Gallagher Convention Centre, Midrand. A few months after that, I had also been a guest at the national elective congress of SASCO in Mangaung, where I had tasted the atmosphere of student politics. It was an atmosphere I wanted to be assimilated into. But I wanted to experience it from within the pan-Africanist movement.

There was a reason I chose to go to Rhodes University, an ivory tower of white supremacy and bourgeois privilege. I had, of course, wanted to be at the University of the Western Cape, among progressive minds. Yet my decision to go to Rhodes University was influenced by my newfound belief that if institutions of higher learning in our country are to be transformed, there is a need for radical minds to be in the belly of the beast where transformation is still only a rumour. I posed an argument to my mother that being at a transformed university would be futile as there was no work that needed to be done there. What was needed was to be where transformation was being resisted and influence that space. I had been a young and naïve eighteen-year-old when I went to Stellenbosch University and had bolted because of the lack of transformation within the institution. But I was twenty-one now, wiser and more courageous. I was prepared to take on the system of white domination that was crippling black students in our liberal universities.

I arrived at Rhodes with great expectations. I knew that it was a liberal institution and, as such, I expected that there would be some element of depoliticisation of students. But what I found there shocked me beyond measure. Not only was Rhodes University extremely liberal, it was also far more depoliticised than I had imagined. Hardly any political formations existed and those that did were rendered irrelevant by the apolitical atmosphere of the institution. The Progressive Youth Alliance, which is comprised of the ANCYL, the Young Communist League of South Africa and SASCO as the leader, had no presence at all. There was no pan-Africanist or Black Consciousness-leaning student political formation. Not a single one. Hardly any students even knew or cared to know about student politics.

There were various academic, cultural and sports societies, most of which I found very reactionary. Examples of these are the Zimbabwean Society (ZimSoc), the Zulu Society, the Lesotho Society (LeSoc) and the Xhosa Society. I found the existence of these societies to be very fragmenting to the student body and the African struggle that confronts our continent. I also felt that Rhodes University was not nurturing cultural diversity but was rather creating fertile grounds for tribalism within the institution. This frustrated me greatly and I was determined to wage a battle against it.

Realising that there was no political student organisation besides those of the Progressive Youth Alliance (PYA), which was made up of three component structures of the ANC-led Mass Democratic Movement and which I couldn't join because they were not pan-Africanist in posture, I decided that I would not be part of any political movement until such time I was able to establish a Black Consciousness organisation on campus. I knew that this would prove to be a herculean task because of the liberal nature of Rhodes University. Most of the students at the university were from a middle-class background, including the black population. As a result of this, it was very difficult to mobilise them into a formidable force, particularly around political matters, as I wanted to do.

My frustrations with the black middle class were born at Rhodes University. I didn't harbour much contempt for this section of our society until I was directly confronted with the extent to which middle class socialisation is detrimental to the waging of serious struggles aimed at bettering the lives of our people. Seeing so many black students being apathetic to the plight of those coming from a working-class background made me understand how when a black child is raised in an environment where they are not taught the importance of struggle they become detached from the existing realities of natives, realities I believe should occupy the minds of all black people in our country.

Having grown up in a township where the sense of community was great, I could not comprehend what inspired the complete desensitisation of the middle-class black population at the university.

I decided I would contribute to the politicisation of Rhodes University by establishing a society in the form of a book club that would focus solely on African literature. I spoke to a few students about launching this society and knew immediately it would fail. Most students, even those who expressed a little enthusiasm, were simply not sold on the idea of having a society that would be regarded as 'racist'. This left me feeling extremely dejected and defeated. I wanted a radical political home. I wanted to be a student activist but, as I've said, I didn't want to join the PYA.

I had a decision to make. I would either continue not being an activist or I could form a political organisation, which, looking at the state of the institution and its extreme liberalism, would be almost impossible. One other option remained: to join SASCO and contribute to its revival. I had attended its national elective conference as a guest in Mangaung the year before and knew deep down that despite its relationship with the ANC, SASCO was a very progressive organisation whose autonomy made allowance for it to have a contradictory relationship with the ruling party. I rationalised this in my head for a very long time until finally, in September, I submitted my membership application form to the organisation.

Joining the South African Students Congress was, I felt, a very brave decision on my part. For many years, I'd been violently opposed to participating in politics of the Congress Movement, and had been hell-bent on seeking an alternative. But I finally succumbed to the pressure of the reality of the situation: that there was no student movement in the country with the power and potential of SASCO, even in a liberal and apathetic institution such as Rhodes University. We had a greater chance at winning victories for the working-class student with SASCO than we did with any other organisation, and to deny this truth would be to swim in an ocean of naivety. In very many ways, SASCO represented everything I detested about you. The organisation had traits typical of the Mass Democratic Movement that we had come to know in the democratic dispensation. The politics of slates, factions and power-mongering were rife, even at branch level. Two months after I joined SASCO, I was elected as the branch secretary following a controversial Annual General Meeting. The AGM was the third to sit after two others before it had been collapsed by the then sitting branch leadership, who didn't want to cede power.

My election into the Branch Executive Committee of SASCO had it advantages. I was finally able to understand how the basic unit of an organisation operates. It gave me useful experience.

But in December 2012, I tended my resignation to SASCO following the outcome of your national elective congress held in Mangaung. I had known for some time that being a member of SASCO meant that I would have to campaign for you in the elections. But it was only after the Mangaung congress that I realised the deeper meaning of this matter: I was going to have to campaign young people in our country and tell them about the vision and mission of an organisation that I could not find it in myself to truly believe in. I was going to go against what I believed in, in the name of organisational discipline. I was going to tell my peers that there was hope yet for our country, and that this hope lay in the hands of an ANC under a leadership I didn't believe was even capable of running a spaza shop in some secluded rural area. As hard as I tried, I couldn't make myself do it. I was incapable of such deceit.

Malaika, Economic Freedom Fighter

In June 2013, I received a message from Floyd Shivambu, the suspended former national spokesperson for the ANC Youth League, requesting a meeting about the formation of a new movement to be led by Julius Malema. I was excited beyond measure! A week or two before receiving the message I'd done an interview with a blog called ZAGossip, for a feature called '30 Under 30 Young Africans You Need to Know'. One of the questions had been: What would you do if you were Julius Malema for the day? My response had been, 'If I were Malema for a day I would form a new political organisation and get Malaika Wa Azania to be its spokesperson. I respect and admire Malema greatly . . .'

I met with comrades Julius and Floyd at the Hector Pieterson Square in Orlando West, Soweto. We met at Nambitha Restaurant on the famous Vilakazi Street to discuss the way forward with this great idea.

I was meeting comrade Julius for the first time in my life! I had seen him at the ANC Youth League congress two years previously. We'd actually sat very close to each other at the VIP afterparty, to which a close friend of mine, Mojalefa, had taken me along as his partner. But I hadn't given in to my temptation to walk up to him and start a conversation.

The meeting at Nambitha was informal and very brief. We agreed that the formation of a radical youth-led movement was a vital necessity in our country and that there was none better suited than comrade Julius, a man who many young people in our country identified with, to lead it. I made it clear from the very beginning that I had no desire to lead a movement but would want to work for the communications and public relations committee, as that is where my strength lies. I was under no illusion about my capacity. I knew I wasn't ready to lead an organisation at a very senior level; at twenty-one years old I had a lot of time to learn and grow within the movement before I could even entertain ambitions of leading in its national steering committee.

Our first task, we decided, was to mobilise as many people as we could in preparation for a consultative forum in which we would decide the orientation and posture of the movement.

We had not determined whether the movement was going to operate within the civic space or whether it was going to become a political party and contest state power. It was a decision we wanted to leave to other stakeholders. In retrospect, I realise that comrades Julius and Floyd were dishonest with me from the very beginning. I have come to believe that they always intended for the movement to be a political party, registered with the Independent Electoral Commission in time for the 2014 national general elections. They wanted me to believe that this decision would be a product of a consultative forum so I'd continue working under the impression that I was doing it for our people, as opposed to helping drive a vehicle intended to settle scores I knew nothing about.

We hit the ground running. From that very day, the mobilisation drive begun on social networks. We created Twitter and Facebook accounts and encouraged people to register as volunteers for the movement. The response was overwhelming. In just a few days, thousands of emails and messages poured in. I was glued to my laptop and cellphone, fielding calls and emails from young people all over the country who wanted to be part of the movement. I barely slept. My mother, who didn't trust the intentions of comrade Julius and was violently opposed to my being part of the movement, nevertheless volunteered herself to be my servant. While I sat behind my laptop updating a spreadsheet that was growing minute by minute and answering phone calls, she'd bring me food and refreshments. She'd resigned herself to the reality that with or without her blessings, I was going to be part of this movement. As a parent, she wanted to support my decision even if she didn't agree with it.

The EFF was going to be my personal mission. For a long time in my life I'd been searching for a political home that I felt fully comfortable in. I had disagreed with a great many people over many issues and I had committed myself to ideals that I believed to be noble only to have them blow up right before my eyes, with no prospect of their being salvaged. I wanted to believe that this was going to finally be that political home, that cause I was prepared to give my life to.

Two weeks after the public announcement that the former Youth League president had established a mass movement, we had our very first consultative meeting at Protea Hotel Wanderers in the prestigious suburb of Illovo in Sandton. It was at this meeting that the Economic Freedom Fighters (EFF) as we know it today was born. The meeting was attended by no more than thirty people, Julius's closest and most trusted allies, and some who it was believed would have interests in being part of the EFF. These people included the likes of Kenny Kunene, who has since left the organisation, Mpho Ramakatsa, who at the time was leading a formidable breakaway faction of the ANC in the Free State, and other young people who were either close personal friends of comrade Julius, or leaders of groups such as Friends of the Youth League, which had been established in solidarity with him following his expulsion.

There were only two women at the meeting: myself and another young woman, a leader of the ANC Youth League who, for her own protection, I won't name. Everyone was seated, with comrade Julius standing behind a makeshift podium addressing us and me taking minutes and passing the register around. The meeting was very heated; some people felt that the EFF was threatening to become a movement of angry people without a political programme, while some argued that the only way to legitimise the EFF was to register it as a political organisation. This was the general consensus. Towards the end, comrade Julius asked if we were all in the same boat but received the shock of his life when the other woman, who'd been quiet throughout the meeting, took to the floor and informed us that she would not, under any circumstances, be joining the EFF. Her argument was that she had been born into and raised in your family, the family of the ANC. She had been a member of all component structures of the Mass Democratic Movement, including the South African Students Congress, the Young Communist League, the ANC Youth League and the ANC itself. She was not willing, she told us, to leave you just like that, even though she agreed with the principles of the EFF and the cause it was pursuing.

I was moved by this woman's honesty and the strength of her convictions. She knew she risked incurring the wrath of the men in that room, particularly comrade Julius. But she wasn't prepared to buy face, even in the presence of people with no fondness for the Congress Movement.

Comrade Julius didn't flinch during the woman's lengthy submission. He just stood watching her, absorbing the impact of every word she uttered. But it was evident, to me at least, that he was seething with rage at the woman's audacity to differ in opinion from him. My suspicion would be confirmed months later, when she told me that comrade Julius hadn't spoken to her since that meeting.

Cracks in the EFF began to show a few days later. SASCO, in its usual provocative manner, released a statement condemning the EFF and hurling all kinds of insults at the movement. Comrade Floyd decided we should respond and, because he was busy preparing for his exams, the responsibility became mine. It wasn't difficult. SASCO's statement was filled with glaring inconsistencies and ideologically baseless assertions that anyone could have deconstructed and exposed for the senselessness it was. I responded to the student organisation's infantile arguments and sent the draft to both comrades Floyd and Julius for proofreading. Because I was busy with other EFF work, when the statement was returned to me, I didn't read it in depth but quickly glimpsed over it before giving it the green light for publication on the social network sites. When I logged into Facebook an hour or two later, I found I'd been tagged by comrade Floyd on the statement. There were hundreds of comments and shares. While I didn't get to read them all, I was stunned by the statement itself. What I'd written as a reasonable response to an unreasonable statement had been transformed into something decorated with insults and puerile ranting divorced from substance. The comrades had edited the statement I'd written to include their own personal attacks on SASCO and had taken unnecessary swipes at the ANC leadership. I was livid not only because of the unwarranted editing of the initial statement but also because I didn't want to dismiss what was clearly becoming par for the course: the attacking of the Congress Movement that found expression on any given platform. It was as if, as the EFF, we were incapable of selling ourselves to people without making mention of and insulting the leadership of the ruling party.

It was on the evening of 19 June that I decided the buck had to stop. I loved the EFF but I wasn't willing to compromise my own values of respect and reasonability at the altar of being favoured by either comrade Julius or comrade Floyd. I sent the following email to them both.

Dear comrades

I am writing this e-mail to address an issue that I feel begs to be engaged upon thoroughly between the three of us, as we are the ones responsible for the communication of Economic Freedom Fighters with the rest of the population of our country.

While it is true that it is not possible to engage on any political question of the country without mentioning the ruling party in our government, I am vehemently opposed to the tone in which we speak about the ANC, particularly when making reference to the current administration. I do not believe that it is in any way fruitful or necessary for us to refer to the ANC as ZANC or to make snide remarks about Zulu people. The reality of the situation is that the ANC is not an organisation of Zuma alone. There are millions of working class people who are members and supporters of the ANC, many who may even disagree with his leadership and politics. But once we release statements that attack Zuma, especially in an insulting manner, we achieve nothing else but mobilising them to defend him. This serves us no purpose at all.

Furthermore, you must understand that some of us are not in EFF because we have scores to settle with Zuma, but because we genuinely believe in the struggle for economic freedom. It is both unfair and unprincipled that we should be dragged into your own battles with Zuma, because we neither know about them nor regard them as more important

161

than the cause we have genuinely joined. Many of us in EFF are not bitter and angry ANC members, so we cannot be expected to be happy about being represented collectively by statements that are scathing attacks on the persona of the man. Equally, we believe in the importance of mobilising youth across all racial, tribal and ethnic backgrounds. But once we start making comments like 'I expect you to defend Zuma because you are a Zulu', we are effectively alienating Zulu people from participating in our organisation.

We want to be different from other organisations, and we are. We shall not, therefore, run this organisation like it is a caricature of all the others who are more vocal on insults and quiet on the articulation of their own policies and positions. We cannot, therefore, be spewing venom against an individual as though we have nothing outside of our anger to communicate to the world.

Comrades Julius and Floyd, the two of you must understand right now that EFF is not your organisation. It is not an organisation that exists to serve your own purpose as individuals. It is an organisation that belongs to us young people who are tired of the status quo. We joined it not because we love you, or because we hate Zuma, but because we love this country and we want what is best for it. As Malaika, I refuse to be used to fight political battles of individuals. I am in EFF to fight for a cause and that to me has nothing to do with settling scores with Zuma.

I have expressed my interest in heading the communications department of the organisation. I shall not have my department tainted by what I believe to be insulting and unnecessary. Not by anyone, and that includes the two of you. I take politics seriously, and I believe we must engage intellectually on issues, not this way we are doing. It serves no purpose of the youth. If this is how things must run, then comrades we are not in this for the same reasons and therefore some of us have no space in the EFF.

Regards
Malaika Wa Azania

The email was sent at the beginning of the end of a peaceful working relationship between the comrades and me. I never imagined when I sent it that it would be received in the manner it was. I did think it would anger them to some degree because no one takes kindly to confrontation, even when it is constructive and not malicious. I had also heard from friends and comrades that comrade Julius in particular did not let confrontations go, and that he dealt harshly with those who dared to differ with him in any way. But I believed that both of them knew that my heart was in the right place and that I believed strongly in the EFF.

Comrade Floyd didn't respond to the email, which was rather strange considering I was closer to him than to comrade Julius, and he understood me better. He should have known, and I believe he did, that I was incapable of keeping quiet about what I perceived to be a wrongdoing, no matter who was doing it. But I soon received a response from comrade Malema. The email was very brief but the point it made was very clear: 'You must never talk to me like you are talking to a school boy . . .'

Of course, I didn't take kindly to this. Who did comrade

Julius think he was to expect no one in the organisation to challenge him? Who did he think he was to reduce people to his subordinates who only spoke when spoken to, and only then to agree with him? No one had ever filtered statements that he was making, so it made no sense to me that he thought it prudent that we filter our statements to him. I'd spent my whole life defending my right to be human in the face of white arrogance. There was no way I was going to be reduced to nothingness by comrade Julius, or any other person for that matter. In response, I launched my own missiles:

> *Of course, being only 21 years old, I am younger than both of you. So outside the question of political respect, I also respect you as elders. But that is not a basis or grounds for you to believe that you are justified in wanting to intimidate me into silence by saying that when I disagree with something and raise the argument critically, I am being disrespectful or that I am addressing you like a 'school boy'. It is unwarranted.*
>
> *I agree that we must respect one another. Let that be a principle that is applied between all of us, and not one that must apply unequally.*

Days went by without any communication from either of them. I was growing uneasy about the EFF, not only because a lot of things that were happening were making me question the sincerity of the comrades involved in the movement, but also because I was forced to answer questions I didn't want to find myself having to deal with. I believed in the EFF with every fibre of my being. I believed that through the movement, the black people's cause would triumph. I couldn't bear the thought that the EFF was just another selfish movement begun to create a cult around an individual or help him settle his own scores against you, the ANC.

I continued to do EFF recruitment work until, one afternoon, having cancelled all social engagements, I decided to dedicate ten hours to organisational work. I wanted to respond to emails and messages from the public, as well as determine which interviews from print media the EFF should respond to.

But I wasn't able to access any of our accounts: email, Facebook or Twitter. I wondered how I could be entering the wrong password into all three. After numerous attempts it was very clear that all account login details had been changed. To say I was shocked would be putting it mildly. I couldn't understand why the comrades would do something so vindictive, not only to me but to the organisation. The reality of the situation was that there was information that only I had access to, such as spreadsheets only I had control of. It was senseless to do something like this in an attempt to spite me when I had information so critical to the organisation. It hit me then just how self-serving the people I was dealing with were—they would punish me by punishing an organisation they claimed to genuinely love. I never had any illusions about my importance; I always knew I was easily replaceable. But I couldn't have imagined I'd be forced out of the organisation over a disagreement based not on ideological posture or something that significant, but on tactics of mobilisation.

I had two choices: walk away from the EFF and find myself yet again without a political home, or stay in the organisation and try by any means to make amends with my comrades. I decided I had nothing but my pride to lose if I stayed, and because my pride wasn't more important than the cause we were fighting, I made the decision to reach out to comrades Julius and Floyd, even if it meant apologising. On 24 June, I sent what would be my last message to them.

Comrades

Over the past few days I've been contemplating the contents of the email I sent you last week, berating you for what I regarded as inappropriate and self-serving conduct. I acknowledge that my tone was not correct and that my passion about my own argument may have led me to being unreasonably harsh. I would like to apologise for my tone and the manner in which I addressed you, for looking at it now in hindsight, I realise the same message could have been communicated better.

Again I got no response and a few days later I left for Zimbabwe as part of the SADC Election Observer Mission for the harmonised elections. For the next seven weeks, I concentrated on nothing but my work in Mazowe West with the other members of my team of three: a former police constable from Botswana, ntate Baingapi, and a South African member of parliament, Dr Luyenge. I was in Harare when I read in *The Herald* that the EFF had been registered as a political party. Of course, by then I knew that the EFF was destined to join the list of hundreds of political parties contesting state power. It didn't come as a shock. But I kept thinking to myself over and over again that it would've have been so much better if the EFF had remained a mass movement for a while. Something about party politics in our country does something to even the noblest of causes, something quite on the opposite side of progress.

Immediately after returning from Zimbabwe, following elections that drained the life out of me, I had to travel to the Gambia in West Africa for training of the African Union Youth Charter's ambassador programme. Soon thereafter, upon being appointed as an ambassador for the SADC region by the African Youth Panel, I had to leave South Africa for another three weeks to represent Africa as a special guest at the International Human Rights Festival in Mexico. In October, when my flight landed at OR Tambo International Airport after a gruelling twelve-hour trip from Paris, I knew I'd returned to a different South Africa. This was not a South Africa of people drowning in helplessness and crushed by defeatism. This was a country burning with excitement and hope. Everywhere in the township, young people were wearing bright-red berets with the EFF logo printed on the front. In taxis, on the streets, in the Gautrain, everyone was talking about this new political party that was going to rewrite the narrative of the oppressed.

I turned twenty-two four days later, on 19 October 2013. I'd lived to see the writing of a new chapter in the story of our beautiful country. I was part of the generation that has witnessed the end of our people being oppressed and trapped by the false belief that they owed their eternal gratitude to you, and that there would be none brave enough to take you on. History will tell the story more accurately some day but it will record 2013 as the year in which a rapture tore through occupied Azania, and left in its wake a mass of a new type of fighter.

Epilogue: The ballot, the people's voice

OUR COUNTRY SITS ON THE THRESHOLD of a historic moment. This year marks exactly two decades since the Republic of South Africa held its first democratic elections in 1994. A few weeks from now, we will be going to the polls to elect a ruling government that will take us through the next five years.

But, most importantly to me, I will be voting for the very first time in my life. I have looked forward to this moment for a long time and I can't wait for the day when I put my X next to the party I have a bit more confidence in than all the others. As things stand, I am conflicted about which party is worthy of my vote. Nothing preoccupies my mind at this moment more who I'll be voting for. Each day, I dedicate a few minutes to the question. Deciding who to vote for is not simply a matter of putting an X next to the party you happen to like or one that you are sentimental about. It is much more serious than that, at least in my eyes. When you vote for a party, you vote for the future of your country. You give powers to a few individuals to decide on the fate of millions, some of whom are too young or powerless to speak for themselves. When you vote for a party, you give them the responsibility of guarding the gains of our liberation struggle. You're saying, 'Steve Biko, Robert Sobukwe, Lilian Ngoyi, Solomon Mahlangu, Khotso Seahlolo and many other sons and daughters of the soil died for this country and I want you to ensure that their deaths were not in vain. Protect their legacy, defend their cause.'

Such a herculean task should never be given to anyone incapable of performing it. And so I find that I conclude with more questions than answers. But I will continue to ask myself this question over the next few weeks, and, hopefully, by the time the day of voting comes I will walk into the voting station with confidence and conviction in my decision. I will make a decision that I can defend, and one that one day, I will defend to my as of yet unborn son, Mwalimu, and his cousin Lalibela, as having been a decision born from principle and integrity.

There are many things that I want to tell these two children, Mwalimu and Lalibela. I want to tell them the truth about where their country came from. I want history to have its say. And it will. One day, history will have its say. It will not tell a story of reconciliation and a born-free generation. It will not tell a story of democracy and equality. History will tell the story of families like mine who struggled and continue to struggle, and of many Malaika Wa Azanias: young people born at the dawn of a democratic dispensation who were filled with optimism about a Rainbow Nation that never was. It will tell the story of young black children whose humanity is destroyed by the brutality of life in the township, a modern-day concentration camp where poor black people find little comfort is afforded to them by a system that sucks the hope out of their very hearts. It will tell the story about what it truly means to be black in democratic South Africa: that poverty, destitution and hunger continue to have a black face. History will tell that democracy is just a word when millions of black people are starving, unemployed and landless. But above all, history will tell a story about you, about your genesis from the people's saviour to the albatross hanging around our necks.

I can only hope that when that day comes, my son, my beloved Mwalimu, and my beautiful niece, Lalibela, will not have their own painful experiences to share. I hope that they will be part of a generation of black South African children who are, in every sense of the term, born free.

Aluta continua!

ABOUT THE AUTHOR

MALAIKA WA AZANIA, real name Malaika Lesego Samora Mahlatsi, was born in Meadowlands, Soweto, in 1991, before moving to Dobsonville Extension 2 in her late teens. She is the former branch secretary of the South African Students Congress at Rhodes University, where she is currently doing her second year of study. Malaika is the outgoing secretary general of the African Youth Coalition, an umbrella body of youth civil society organisations affiliated to the Pan African Youth Union. She is currently the African Union African Youth Charter Ambassador for the SADC region and the executive director of her own writing and transcribing company, Pen and Azanian Revolution (Pty) Ltd. In 2012, she founded a pan-Africanist journal, *Afrikan Voices of the Left*, dedicated to the memory of PAC founding president, Robert Sobukwe. Malaika is a published essayist, a blogger, a columnist on *Thought Leader*, *The Sunday Independent* and *DestinyConnect*, a contributor to *The Thinker* magazine, a fierce debater and an activist devoted to pursuing the African Renaissance agenda.

She is currently based in Grahamstown.

SIMPHIWE DANA is a Xhosa singer and songwriter whose distinctive style fuses jazz, Afro-soul, and traditional music. Called "the best thing to happen to Afro-Soul music since Miriam Makeba" by South African media, she is also a prominent activist and the first African ambassador for Amnesty International.

ABOUT SEVEN STORIES PRESS

SEVEN STORIES PRESS is an independent book publisher based in New York City. We publish works of the imagination by such writers as Nelson Algren, Russell Banks, Octavia E. Butler, Ani DiFranco, Assia Djebar, Ariel Dorfman, Coco Fusco, Barry Gifford, Martha Long, Luis Negrón, Peter Plate, Hwang Sok-yong, Lee Stringer, and Kurt Vonnegut, to name a few, together with political titles by voices of conscience, including Subhankar Banerjee, the Boston Women's Health Collective, Noam Chomsky, Angela Y. Davis, Human Rights Watch, Derrick Jensen, Ralph Nader, Loretta Napoleoni, Gary Null, Greg Palast, Project Censored, Barbara Seaman, Alice Walker, Gary Webb, and Howard Zinn, among many others. Seven Stories Press believes publishers have a special responsibility to defend free speech and human rights, and to celebrate the gifts of the human imagination, wherever we can. In 2012 we launched Triangle Square books for young readers with strong social justice and narrative components, telling personal stories of courage and commitment. For additional information, visit www.sevenstories.com.